Functional Literacy for Deprived

By

Dr. (Mrs.) Shashi Kumar

ANMOL PUBLICATIONS PVT. LTD.
NEW DELHI - 110 002 (INDIA)

ANMOL PUBLICATIONS PVT. LTD.
4374/4B, Ansari Road, Daryaganj
New Delhi - 110 002
Ph.: 23261597, 23278000
Visit us at: www.anmolpublications.com

Functional Literacy for Deprived

First Published, 2005

ISBN 81-261-2134-3

PRINTED IN INDIA

Published by J.L. Kumar for Anmol Publications Pvt. Ltd., New Delhi - 110 002 and Printed at Mehra Offset Press, Delhi.

CONTENTS

FOREWORD

Earth is the laboratory where biological and physical processes are experimented and endeavor to improve the quality of life. It warrants a thorough understanding of various earth system processes. Man is the important element of the environmental complexes. His activities, growing population, industrial and urban settlement social religious and economic setups are causing newer ecological problems. In India awakening has begun for humanity to successfully meet the evolutionary and revolutionary challenges. Great cultural achievements of the past must be revised and enriched to bring about a new type of humanity. A society marked by integrated power of physical, emotional, dynamic, intellectual, clinical, esthetic and spiritual potentialities. I fee the need of re-orientation of Home science to human Ecology for the setting where rich and poor can come together to build common understanding to achieve rural development and hunger alleviation goals.

It is heartening to note that Dr. Mrs. Shashi Kumar is addressing the concern of empowerment of women in her book "Functional Literacy for Deprived". I am sure this book would help in understanding the dynamic linkages between gender and development. Women empowerment through community based programmes, especially in the realm of human ecology would go a long way in this direction. I feel this important work would provoke more insights in the policy debate. I hope the book would also be useful for students, civil society community and all other concerned.

Sumitra Mahajan
Member of Parliament (Lok Sabha)

PREFACE

We are looking at the prospects of international prosperity going back to assist in political evolution of the country. Indians feel things have improved and they face the future with an increased confidence. The great challenges of development require an authoritarian hand to nurture democracy. It concerns the debate to nature the reality and the ability of our concepts to represent reality. Modern sciences lack an adequate account of the mind. However, all of us are pilgrims on this earth. Argentine poet Almafuerte wrote "To the weak difficulty is closed door". To the strong however, it is a door waiting to be opened. Difficulties impede the progress of those who are weak. For the strong however, they are opportunities to open wide the doors to a bright future.

The present publication has been specially documented to start the journey to human ecology for the reform of the masses. The main thrust will be directed toward youth employment, income generation and generation of mass awareness about developmental issues. The activities which are socially beneficial and economically viable like on farm, off-farm, and non-farm can be taken up for the benefits to the rural and the urban slum community so that the resources and the environment may be preserved for the future generation.

— **Dr. (Mrs.) SHASHI KUMAR**

CHAPTER 1

Education for Human Resource Development

There is a great demand for expansion of higher education on account of increasing expansion of primary and secondary education and rising social expectation. Consequently emphasis has been on the removal of disparities and to equalise educational opportunities attending specific needs to those who has been on the removal of disparities and to equalise educational opportunities attending to specific needs to those who have been equality so far.

Educational development is participatory process. Education was incorporated in the list to facilitate evolution of all Indian policies in the field of education (Government has assumed a larger responsibility to look after the integrated character of education, to look after international aspects of education, culture and human resource development) in the general to promote excellence in the sectors of education throughout the country. Having regard to the size of population, diversity and economic frailtics the challenges is enormous. This realisation has resulted in steadily rising levels of budgetary allocations, and resource transfer for education to the states.

Elementary Education. Universal access, universal relation and universal achievement are broad parameters to achieve the goal of universalisation of elementary education is yet to be achieved. Considering the magnitude and the complexity of the problem, meticulously formulated strategies to have been adopted in the form of operation blackboard (OB), Non-Formal Education (NFE), Teacher Education (TE), district primary education programme to address the specific problem areas, gender and regional disparities. Special problem areas, gender and regional disparities, special focus has been laid on the access to education for millions of girls and working children, who cannot participate in the school system on account of socio-economic compulsions. These segments largely constitute girls SCs/STs and other deprived sections of the society.

Although special programmes have been taken up to improve upon specific deficiencies in the educational system, no strategies can succeed in achieving UEE without specifically addressing its gender and regional dimensions.

Human Ecology for Women

The status of women in a complex society like ours, is not uniform within the Indian sub-continent, there have been infinite variations of the status of women, different according to the cultural milieu, family structure, caste class, occupation, property rights etc. All these factors are significant determinants of variation in her position in different groups.

The scheduled caste women who constitute a sizable population of India is subjected not merely to gender bias, but also to indignities arising out of age old traditions of untouchability from which, incidentally the entire social group of scheduled castes suffer. The deep-rooted social discriminations have compelled this section of India's population to lead a life of bare subsistence level, both in respect to economic terms and human values. The scheduled caste households are largely rural based. They have tied themselves to land owners — that happens to be from high castes, by a variety of complex relationship to ensure survival. The variety of complex relationship is reflected in a much larger number of scheduled caste farm servants and attached labourers. This very distinction warrants the scheduled caste women agricultural workers to be recognised as a separate social sub-group in the directed empowerment process.

In rural India more than 80% of people are involved directly or indirectly in agricultural and allied activities like animal husbandry, poultry fishery, sericulture mushroom floriculture and a number of other related pursuits. This sector is the mainstay of Indian economy; and nearly 50% of the country wealth if not more, in this share is generated through women.

It is against all oppressive structure. It is all exploitation inside the family and outside. So the alternative development is a people based development and the answers should come from people.

Home Science

The field of home science research is today at the crossroads. Researchers in Human development and family studies are in the process of becoming aware of the need for building indigenous theories, developing their own tools and experimenting with research designs and methods of investigation most suited for the study of human behaviour in the Indian cultural context. With its long history of involvement and commitment to the cause of children, women and families, it was felt that the department has a moral responsibility to respond to the need to think of ways to strengthen the interface among research public policy and programmes. For conducting studies on women agriculture and rural extension :

1. What facts do researchers in human development and family studies have to offer policy and programme planners?

2. How can information be most effectively reached to these agencies?
3. What modifications are needed in the approach to research in Human Development and Family Studies, to make it more socially relevant and useful?
4. What is the role of human development and family studies research in social development?

This shall support :

- To revitalise their curriculum in human development and family studies
- To plan relevant and meaningful research for their institutions
- Lacunae in research that need investigation on a priority basis.

The need for translating the research funding of child development and other allied disciplines into a language and format that can be accepted by policy planners has also been stated. Several themes which reflect common concerns and point to future agenda and course of action for researchers in human development and family studies and allied disciplines.

Finally, a very important that has emerged is that of setting up an interdisciplinary task force in Early Childhood Care and Education. Its function will be tu prepare a research agenda, and play a leadership role by evolving a comprehensive framework to guide research efforts of various institutions across the country; monitor the translation of research findings to policy and programme and coordinate the effective dissemination of information between and among programme and policy planners, and other relevant agencies and the general public.

As one who has in a small way been instrumental in shaping the destiny of this institution during its formative years, to give me great satisfaction and a sense of immense pride in having your kind support for the cause of humanity.

World conferences on women have invariably aroused worldwide enthusiasm and awareness amongst all quarters concerned with gender issues. In our own country and have been acted as prime mover to initiate and promote very many innovative policies and programmes to bring about gender equity, equality and justice. The fourth world conference at Beijing in September 1995 was momentous. The Indian publications on women's issues have come a long way from a small shelf of books on the status of women, into a library of a wide range of collection on women's issues, women's rights, laws, cultural and social issues, employment and labour aspects, poverty and economic issues, and to mention a few. A brief review of the study made on reproductive health care of women in Delhi slums, it was found that as far as the prenatal care was concerned less than 33% of women could utilise it, because they were not aware of such service. Thus it was disappointing to find that information was not percolating down to the grass-root level and the claims of awareness generation by official machinery were not wholly true. If such was the situation right under the nose of the government in Delhi slums, one could imagine the condition in rural areas and other remote places. So far as the educational level of women in the areas studied is concerned, a sample survey of about 500 women in reproductive age of 15 to 40 years was made. It was found that only 22% of these women were literate as against Delhi Literacy rate of 67%.

Population and food raise many questions for human race. This reflects the compelling interest, which especially seeks to establish links with other intellectual disciplines such as philosophy history and social sciences.

Modern ecological studies have been increasingly directed towards measuring the productivity of various kinds of ecosystems and to determining the factors that influence it. When plant material is eaten by herbivorous animals roughly only about 10% is transfer into carnivore tissue, we thus arrive at the idea of a chain each stage of which represents a loss of energy of 90-95 per cent and this leads us to well-known pyramid of numbers which is to be found in ecosystem and to the concept of primary and higher order of secondary produces, ecologists now presents their a loss of energy of 90 to 95% and this leads us to well-known pyramid of numbers which is to be found in ecosystem and to the concept of primary and higher order of secondary producers, ecologists now present their information in terms of bio-mass of total weight of living organisms involved.

Rural household and farming systems have become prime focus of development assistance in recent years. Both in applied research and project work a farm family perspective has been adopted to achieve successful agricultural development.

The farm is no longer viewed solely as a production unit. The focus has shifted to the rural household in its relation to its socio-economic and cultural environment.

The rural family is seen as a central decision making unit for the utilisation of existing development potential and the application of innovations. Simultaneously, the rural household accounts for social stability in the society and for securing the material and non-material essential needs of individual members.

The peasant household is seen as the central decision making unit in rural development. This refers not only to utilisation of existing development potentials, the implementation of development measures of the introduction of innovation of various kinds but also social stability in the society and to the satisfaction of material and non material needs of its individual members.

Legal and political impediments to Gender Quality for women.

Among the developing countries of Asia, India remains an interesting case study for investigation into variety of analytical issues related to emerging gender structure. Women constitute nearly fifty per cent of the total population of our country and yet the participation rate of women in decision making levels very low. Despite the constitutional provisions and other legislative measures, policy guidelines and programmes and projects, the inequality of opportunity unequal access to material resources of greater number of women, especially the working women, still persists in a large measure.

As we approach the 21st century the eyes of the world are turned towards Asia characterised by rapid economic growth, an unmatched diversity of political and economic systems and a kaleidoscope of people, culture and religions, the region offers the most interesting field for understanding the location of 'gender' of women as well as for seeking means for redressing gender inequality.

Asia is the fastest growing regions of the world in terms of GDP while it holds dramatic diversity with respect to economic growth impulses and strategies, it has a building unity in its cultural roots and modes-offering a veritable laboratory to understand the play of different models of growth on the social fabric. Asia is a varied experience form the G-7 Japan at one end; to the east Asian export led growth success; the incredible, awakening out of one political economy model at another resounding success; to the poverty bowl-south Asia at the other end.

Economic growth and greater influence in the global

arena have been achieved at a heavy price. Poverty and inequality in Asia is growing. Asia's culturally strong society is being transformed into more typically agitated society characterised by the strong scars of civic restlessness, a deterioration in women's position in increasing violence, especially against women.

India will march a head if grass-root workers are given the opportunity for decentralised efforts. Village level activists, to handle the responsibility entrusted to them to the cause of rural women and children. Notwithstanding their handicap of little or lack of education, in fact we have found them to be experienced and articulate in the rural context.

We also found that farm women is highly committed to their duties and women's welfare. Even though they operate in a dispersed set up. They work in unison with one another in implementing the state policy on women and children, which is entreated to them. The exposure, training and support structure provided them not only has enthused to work efficiently and effectively but also help them in shedding their traditional inhibitions and this awakening amongst the farm women and girls with whom they come in contact. Thus they are working as catalysts and change against in the village.

An overall assessment suggests that the effort case with which the women could mobilise women for social change was neither offensive nor unwelcome by the village community, barring some case prejudices here and there. New awakening amongst the rural women folk will indirectly be a very supportive awareness to the Panchayati Raj. In fact women can be great aid and ally to the Panchayati Raj movement in different districts and states. Therefore, we feel that the change, that both government and non-governmental organisation expected from the educated members and workers of social welfare the village women may be called partners can exert their innate potential for the good of the people. The social and community problems cannot be triad carbonate. As part and parcel of the community a village woman's ability to ingratiate herself within the villagers to introduce social change, is a significant landmark in the history to community.

Social welfare is as old as humanity itself. Helping the needy and the person in distress has been in existence particularly in all the civilisation communities. From time immemorial, social welfare has recently developed into a scientific programme for poverty, sickness suffering, social degradation have always been known to man in long course of history' of mankind, but after the industrial revolution new social problems were erased, which could not be faced by the older human institutions-family, neighbourhood and local community. In fact this was not the situation only in industrial societies particularly in the wet, but such a situation is being created in the developing countries also. Apart from the humantarian aspect, the development of scientific knowledge provided the tools for investigating the causes of poverty, of human deficiencies and dissatisfaction with the sole object to find out a remedy for various social problems facing the society. Hence social welfare development into a scientific concept based on a scientific knowledge of the problems facing the society, particularly in free society with the object of finding out ways and means of solving these problems.

The concept of service of one's fellow men has been an integral part of Indian traditions. The ruptures shared the responsibilities of meeting the needs of the individuals and groups in difficulties, the rich and the members of the general community shared the individuals and the group's difficulty. Religion institutions also played a very important part in providing social service. We come across men and women and group of persons who devote their lives to the service of helpless. The measures of goodwill and some leisure time with the industrialisation and urbanisation, our social problems are becoming more and more complex. There is also a growing recognition that for handling such complex social problems of social, economic and human relationship, we require certain technical knowledge concerning human behaviour, social institutions etc.

Thus understanding of social relationship, social psychology and social economics has helped to understand the social problems and the ways and means of organising social welfare services on scientific basis with the help of a tested body of knowledge. An orphan child needs more than food and clothing in children's institution. The problems of aged and infirm persons are partly social and partly psychological in nature. Therefore, the institutions of this basic human needs. There is a need for social welfare programmes like balwadis, holiday homes, youth hostels etc. which help in the prevention of occurrence of social problems. The programmes of social assistance have also to play a very important part in building up the human material. Various services like creche, orphanages, and homes for the blind, workshops of the orthopedically handicapped persons, community welfare contract were set up by the interested citizens for the purpose of providing welfare services to the needy and the destitute.

Whereas, there has been a large measure of goodwill and dedication, there has been dearth of technical knowledge required to run various welfare services. Foreign literature was available on various social welfare services but this was not suited to the requirements of Indian condition. Attempts have been Made in certain areas of welfare, work to provide material on different kinds of social welfare service, like minimum standards on child care institutions, worked out by the Indian conference of social work, and the minimum standards for different welfare programmes by the central social welfare board etc. some useful material is also available from the reports of various committees and proceedings of conference and seminars on social legislation. All this material is not only inadequate but is not available to the social workers in one place.

Attempts have been made in certain areas of work but this was not suited to the requirements of Indian conditions. Dedication of service towards one's fellowmen, love for charity and brotherhood existed even in times religion emphasised the values of charity philanthropy and mutual help. Indian history revert that the responsibility of assessing the individual in need was hired by the community and the rulers. During the period of King Ashoka one reads about the appointment of Gopas who were supposed to keep the records of caste, gotra, occupation births, deaths, marriage etc. The duties of gopas were akin to modern social workers. The king took more and more responsibility towards providing social services to the public. During the early British period the impact of education and economic the reformers fought for equality of rights for women and abolition of widow re-marriage. The voluntary organisation like Arya Mahila Samaj, Anjuman-e-Himayat-e-Islam, Ramkrishana Mission, Theosophical society, Servants of India society and a large number of Christian missionaries contributed considerably to the provision of welfare services for the needy and the handicapped.

These traditions of social services were influenced by various social and economic factors. The social institutions like the joint family, the caste system and the village panchayats provided mechanism, which would meet the needs of the sick, the aged, the destitute and the handicapped members of the community. Industrialisation and urbanisation also changed the pattern of life. New social problems cropped up, for the solution of which the existing social institutions found themselves ineffective. Without the development of social science it beacon possible to make a systematic study if the social problems in order to solve these on a comprehensive and scientific basis. We, therefore, started moving is nonbeing laid on the application of scientific methods to the solution of social problems *i.e.* by studying the social and economic factors of the problem and acquiring special skills and techniques, in dealing with them.

Social welfare board. Social welfare services were brought on the political map of India in 1953 with the setting up of the central social welfare as a part of first five year plan. During the recent years there has been increasing realisation that with a view to improving and preserving the human capital which is one of the most important factors of production of any economic development. It is necessary to provide opportunities for growth and development of the child. The social welfare field has so far been a combination of various social welfare activities without aiming at an integrated approach either to the child or to a family or to the community.

Voluntary agencies. Voluntary welfare organisations have been rendering useful service in the past and sharing the burden of welfare services of the state. In many areas they have playing pioneering role in providing relief and assistance to the people in distress. Many of the agencies are a century old now occasionally financial assistance helps the organisations to expand their programmes, But the absence of continued help and outmoded methods of collecting funds impede the planned development of social welfare in the voluntary sector. Coupled with these difficulties in the dearth of voluntary welfare workers are now going away from the beneficiaries and bureaucracy is also entering into voluntary agencies. The voluntary workers with a few exceptions are no longer able to provide human touch for which they were known.

With changing needs due to changes in social and economic system, there is need to reorient the methods of provided services by the voluntary agencies or organise social services on certain minimum standards. This has not been possible so far. The central social welfare board has decided to create machinery for field counselling service to assist and guide the welfare organisations in improving the standard of their services.

Social security measures. Various field of social welfare pertaining to children, women and aged and infirm handicapped and various other community welfare services, etc., there are still many gaps and weak points in social welfare activities in this country. For the development of the human material it is necessary to link social welfare programmes with the programmes of social services, and social security which is still infancy in this country.

Child welfare. In order to preserve and to improve human capital, investment in the child is very important, in any plan of economic development. The child should be looked after as much as look after our dams, factories etc. and that in many welfare programmes priority should be given for meeting the basic needs of child. These needs are healthful food adequate clotting, comfortable home with love and understanding, educational facilities, healthy services recreational activities etc., In order to satisfy these needs, the child should be looked after as much as we look after our dams etc. and that in any welfare programmes priority should be provided with all basic services necessary for its physical, mental, emotional and intellectual growth. As investment in basic preventive services for the child is a must in order to prevent blindness, deafness, mental illness or other social handicaps. This will minimise expenditure on the services meant for the treatment of these social ills. These services must be coordinated and integrated so that the total needs of children are met and we have a complete child physically, mentally, and intellectually strong. It may not be possible at this stage to provide all these services to the entire child population in age group of 0-16 but it is necessary to make start somewhere. The Government of India worked on this principle and have initiated demonstration projects of integrated child welfare services in similar community so that all the needs of child are met on integrated comprehensive basis, methods adopted and the results achieved are demonstrated to the community so that the programmes could spread in future.

Human Ecology for Globalisation

When the world and inevitably India are in the throes of major social, economic and technological change, the process will affect the market economy of the nation and also the whole system of higher education. The system has to prepare its graduates for participation in the social economic development of the country, and type of cultural environment and ethic it will need to foster. Information technology is further contributing to this change and will have a major impact on structure, management, and mode of delivery of the educational system.

To develop basic theoretical understanding of discipline but that the understanding should relate to its operational implications for application on making theory-practice an integrated whole in the area of the discipline. The traditional courses should also be encouraged to provide regular field placement of the students to have a "hands on" experience. Due to regional imbalances universities and institutes are developing programmes, which focus on access to quality development of the university/institutes, and colleges located in such regions should receive special attention to the university/ institute and the college in backward areas. The expectation is that the universities will also develop greater emphasis to project greater relevance to societal need and legitimise its public support through reaching out to the more disadvantaged groups by undertaking field outreach activities.

These activities should be for undertaking social change functions with respect to women's studies. The centre should be essentially interdisciplinary and headed by a professor/ reader with teaching and/or research experience in the area of women's studies and other extension/field action experiences. UGC should deliberate on academic matters of common interest for development of higher education. The contribution of higher education to national development of backward areas. UGC decided on 26th March 1996 at the meeting of commission that no university will be allowed to enroll candidates for one sitting for the BA degree courses from the academic year 1996-1997 onwards. There were 214 universities and deemed universities including 27 agricultural universities, 2 veterinary universities, 4 medical universities and 2 technological universities with the affiliated colleges constituting the target segment of the higher institutions of higher education, the total teaching staff in the universities and affiliated colleges was 3.21 lakhs as against 3.10 lakhs in the previous year.

We are a country of rich heritage. Our culture accorded a high position to women in society. It is unfortunate that over the years the very security that was built for women became a barrier for their advancement and deprived them of education and confined them to home. We now have the opportunity to show the world how this trend can be reversed and women accorded an equal status with men.

PARTNERSHIP FOR SUSTAINABLE DEVELOPMENT

In the present age, when every one is aware of the importance of sustainable environment, training the mass in environment management is the need of hours. It is necessary to change people's attitude with regard to environment. A new environmental behaviour is necessary in which quantitative demands and qualitative appreciation and coordination must replace confrontation. This will hopefully lead us into new era of human harmony where all care for well-being of life on earth.

Deterioration of environment tends compelling weight to the need to find a balance between human development and exploitation of natural resources. Some people still claim that the environmental alerts are somewhat exaggerated. The world's population must be limited in the struggle for survival. Department of environmental efficient technology, participation of individual, and change in our thinking and behaviour should help guide us to a sustainable path to ecological stability, bearing in mind that equity and justice ought to prevail with in and between human generations.

The concept of human development is much and richer than what can be captured, simple tool is needed. HDI reflects achievements in the most basic human capabilities — leading of long life knowledgeable and enjoying decent standard of living. These three variables have been chosen to represent that dimension :

- Life expectancy, educational attainment and income
- Show the improvement in methodology and data can affect country's ranking.
- Deprivation in knowledge by illiteracy and deprivation in income between ethnic groups, man and women, in political and professional life.

New information opens people's lives to culture and all its creativity — and to the flow of ideas and knowledge. Today's flow of culture is unbalance, heavily weighted in one direction from rich country to poor. Weightless good with high knowledge contents rather than material contents. Foreign culture can out cultural diversity identity. What is needed is support to indigenous and national cultures with the cost of communications and innovative tools easier to use, people around the world have burst into conversation.

Fundamental rethinking of policy and governance is again required; the key priorities :

- Putting human concern and human rights at the centre of national policy and action.
- Reform driven by concern for people, not for capital
- Development priorities for people for poverty reduction, equity, sustainability and human development.

Globalisation offers great opportunities for human advances — Global markets, global technology, global ideas and global solidarity can enrich the lives of people everywhere. The challenges are to ensure that the benefits are shared — An agenda market place and translate them in more equable into human advances with a human face. The growing interdependent of people's lives call for values and shared commitment to human development of all people — but only with stronger governance — local, national, regional and global — to preserve the advantages of global markets competition, but also to provide enough space for human community and environmental resources to ensure that globalisation works for people — not for profits, globalisation with ethics, equity, inclusion, human security, sustainability and development.

Globalisation is often described as a natural phenomena. However, globalisation is not inevitable. There is not one but many alternatives to globalisation based on the rights of people rather than the rights of corporations, based on democracy rather than corporate rule.

Globalisation is a political process, which has been forced on the weak by the powerful through political institutions such as the Structural Adjustment projects of the World Bank and IMF and the free-trade arrangements of the World Trade Organisation.

Globalisation is not new. It was earlier simply called colonialism. The first wave was the colonisation of the Americans, Africa, Asia and Australia by European powers over 500 years. The first free-trade treaty was a treaty between the East India Company and the declining Moghul Empire in India.

Globalisation is basically a take over of the rights of citizens by corporations through a dismantling of the structures of the state that protect people. It is, therefore, leading to less freedom for people, but more freedom for capital. The search for absolute freedom by corporations is expressed in the rules of the Multilateral Agreement for Investment being negotiated by the OECD, to then be imposed on the rest of the world.

The growth under globalisation is not a growth in goods and services, but a growth in international trade and a growth of the financial economy. For the poorest of the world increased free trade internationally leads to an increase in poverty by the diversion of or destruction of the resources on which they survive and by the dismantling of institutions which protect their rights.

Materially emptied cultures are then pitted against one another, because their common economic base has disappeared. Cultural diversity is then pushed into conflict. Globalisation will protect the environment by leading to economic growth and hence creating more resources for environmental resources and a greater appreciation of environmental values. This assumes that only the rich are environmentally aware. The movements of women, peasants, small fish workers, indigenous people and tribals for environmental protection empirically falsify the assumption. Globalisation is increasing violence and disintegration in society by increasing economic insecurity and by ethnicising and ghettoising all forms of dissent, protect and articulation of alternatives.

Capital is defined as a source of freedom, but this freedom is based on the denial of freedom to the land, forests, rivers and biodiversity that capital claims as its own and to others whose rights are based on their labour. Because property obtained through privatisation of commons is perceived to be depriving the owner of capital of freedom. Thus peasants and tribals who demand the return of their rights and access to resources are regarded as thieves. It seems that the western powers are still driven by colonizing impulse to discover, conquer own and possess everything, every society, and every culture. The colonies have now been extended to the interior spaces the entice codes of life forms from microbes and plants to animals including humans.

Today's patents have a continuity with the patents issued to Columbus. The conflicts that have been unleashed by the GATT treaty, by patents on life forms, by the patenting of indigenous knowledge and by genetic engineering are grounded in processes that can be summarised and symbolised as the second coming of Columbus. At the heart of the Columbus discovery was the treatment of piracy as a natural right of coloniser and necessary for the development of the third world communities.

Through patents and genetic new colonies are being carved out. The land, the forests, the rivers, the oceans, the atmosphere have all been colonised, eroded, and polluted. Capital now has to look for new colonies to invade and exploit for its further accumulation. These new colonies are, in my view the interior spaces of the bodies of women, plants and animals. Resistance to Biopiracy is a resistance to this ultimate colonisation of life itself — of the future evolution as well as the part and future of non-western traditions of relating nature and knowing nature.

Globalisation is not the cross cultural interaction of diverse societies it is the imposition of particular culture on all others.

Nor is globalisation the search for ecological balance on a planetary scale. It is perdition of one class, one race and often one gender of a simple species on all others. The "global" in the dominant discourse is the political space in which the dominant local seeks global control, and frees itself of local, natural and global control and responsibility and limits arising from the imperatives of ecological sustainability and social justice. The global in this sense does not represent the universal human interest; it represents a particular local and parochial interest and culture, which has been globalised through its reach and control, its irresponsibility and lack of reciprocity.

When the rights of farmers to save, exchange, evolve seed are denied, when the rights of consumers to safe and adequate food is denied, what we have is totalitarianism of a most basic kind since it is a totalitarianism based on the total control over the vital necessity — food.

How do we build alternatives in the context of this totalitarianism of a new kind — a totalitarianism based on the rule of fictions rather than the gun boat, a totalitarianism built on dispensability of the majority rather than their bondage, a totalitarianism in which there is no dictator, no person, no government, but all pervading corporations which are themselves a legal fiction?

Rejuvenating our knowledge and skills to meet our needs with our own resources, and our own capacities is the alternative to the monopoly on life inherent to patents on life. The Third World people and women have from the beginning of the waves of globalisation have had to organise ourselves again and again to define our presented so that we too could govern ourselves, fulfil our humanity, defend our community and other species. We know what it is like to excluded. We need to remember how we have organised in the past, how we have built democratic institutions and cultures. Corporate rules have excluded all people as persons.

Diversity is intimately linked to the possibility of self-organisation. It is, therefore, the basis of both Swadeshi and Swarj of economic and political freedom.

Decentralisation and local democratic control are political corollaries of the cultivation of diversity. Peace is also derived from conditions in which diverse species and communities have the freedom to self-organise and evolve according to their own needs, strictures and priorities.

Living societies, living ecosystems, living organisms are characterised by three principles :

(a) the principle of diversity.

(b) the principal of self-organisation, self-regulation, self renewal.

(c) the principle of reciprocity between systems, which is also called the law of return.

Our diversity makes mutuality and a critique of give and take possible. Mutuality makes self-organisation possible. There are two conflicting paradigms of biodiversity. Local communities, whose survival and sustenance is linked to biodiversity utilisation and conservation, hold the first paradigm. Commercial interests, whose profits are linked to utilisation of global biodiversity for production of inputs into large scale, homogeneous, uniform centralised and global production systems hold the second.

The educational philosophy of the university gets translated into its somewhat unorthodox academic structure. Grounded in a faith in the unity of knowledge, department structure of the conventional universities, preferring instead to bring allied disciplines within a few broad and inclusive parameters called schools under whose interactive ambit are placed the more specialised units called centres. At the Master's level, where most of the schools begin their academic programme, training is largely oriented towards single discipline. At the research level it is the development of research solutions that the going becomes precarious. A series of regional workshops that have focused on linkages between research and development. Certainly the linkages are not near and certainly the processes that give the utilisation of research are complex phenomena that are not completely understood. The problems associated with the practical application of university based research have been taken place in Latin America, North Africa and the Middle East, Eastern and Southern Africa have had a special focus on the problems associated with practical application be brought into line with the real needs of agricultural communities. Understanding the world beyond the research system countries to be one of the principle objective. Parallel efforts will be undertaken to ensure that these technologies are brought to bear with in the context of the user themselves and resources will be directed towards increasing the effectiveness of research.

As such research utilisation programme has been designed with three main pillars. The first will be the sub programme on applied R & D systems. The thirst of this initiative will be to understand better R & D from a system perspective. Failures in the transfer of technology may not be solely attributable to the transfer itself. It is possible that there is a failure in research design, or that there is a system failure. Activities relating to commercialisation of research, with in a particular client/market orientation will from the core of this sub programme. The second sub-programme will focus on institutionalisation capabilities for research application. Here the principle objective will be to built and strengthen the capabilities of research and research supporting institutions to engage in activities related to development for creation of communication of infrastructure network.

The growth of India's agriculture during the past nearly

100 years is closely linked with the researchers done and technologies generated. As a centre of higher education and training in agricultural sciences at national and international level :

- To conduct basic and strategic researches with a view of understanding the processes, in all their complexity and to undertake need based research and sustained agricultural productivity in harmony with the environment.
- To serve as a centre for academic excellence in the area of postgraduate education and human resource development in agricultural sciences.
- To provide national leadership in agricultural research, extension and technology assessment and transfer by developing new concepts and approaches and serving as a national referral point for quality and standards.
- To develop information systems, add value to information share and serve the information nationally and serve as a data base.

Linkages and Collaborations

For the national leadership in all major agricultural research areas, IARI has close linkages with almost all annual crops and horti crops research institutes, centres, project directorates, coordinated project, as well as few selected institutes of ICAR; similar linkages exist for natural resource and socio-economic research institutes; collaboration exists with almost all state agricultural universities (SAUs).

Institutional Setting

To supporting and promoting research the task of activising diverse partners in a network of necessity is certainly a challenge for students of organisational design. Indian agricultural research efforts has three institutional basis :

SAU system, ICAR and the private industry The last is yet to carve a niche for it self.

The SAU system consists of 26 universities, at least one in each state. Some state have more than one *e.g.*, Maharashtra and Uttar Pradesh. SAU's have admission capacity of over 1400 undergraduates and nearly 5000 postgraduates while the SAU concept owes much to the US Land Grant college model. The university education commission perhaps described the need rather well catering for the establishment of rural colleges and universities where no field of human concern should be foreign to them.

The SAU system has about 19,000 scientists engaged in education, research and extension activities. The agricultural university concept was based on the need for a project in which research teaching and extension would be fully integrated and geared towards solving the felt need of the farmers. ICAR and SAU work together supporting each other's activities. The relationships are complex and for our purpose it may be worth nothing that SAU are state Government institution while ICAR is central in character.

Agriculture research in India is a mega effort. A vast network of teaching, research and extension groups with such competence employed in solving fanners problems, the productivity in Indian agriculture should have been better than what it is. A large volume of research solutions to farmers' problems is made available to the community but a few are accepted. The fault may be inadequacy of solution, the transfer mechanism, the limitations of the understanding of the adopters; all or some of them to check the systems of faults and leakage

- Are we conformable in managing such a mega system
- Does the size itself post its unique problems of reduction to put it bluntly; can the civil service

system foster a culture of innovation where age and seniority are not at advantage.

Management of research seems to be as important as the research activity itself in Indian agriculture. These problems are of motivation of achieving excellence and coping with externalities.

TOWARDS SUSTAINABLE COMMUNITIES

Action Mechanism for Conservation of Global Biodiversity Education

India recognises the new global scenario poses unprecedented challenges for the higher education system. The university grants commission has appropriately stated that whole range of skill will be demanded from the graduates of humanities, social sciences, natural sciences and commerce as well as from the various professional disciplines such as agriculture law management or engineering.

India can no longer continue the model of general education as it has been persisting in for large bulk of student population. Rather, it requires a major investments to make human resource productive by compiling the older general disciplines of humanities, social sciences and commerce to their applications in the new economy having adequate field based experience to enhance knowledge with skill and develop appropriate attitudes.

International Cooperation

To adopt the new information society technologies such as distance education and internet to forestall the further widening the gap seen in the context of partnership by sharing their successful experience and technologies, material and financial resources and learning to appreciate each other's cultural heritage marked by integrated powers bound to expand new researches to arrive at new equations and new combination. However, it is essential to consider the specific national environment of user and to adopt training material to local situation to ensure their suitability in different context. The HRD movement through new HRD departments to look after or appointed HRD managers to take initiative to strengthen their personal departments.

CHAPTER 2

WOMEN'S COMPONENT PLAN

Introduction

Stepping into the 21st century, India can legitimately take pride in the remarkable progress it has made in every area of human endeavour over the last five decades. Synergy between science, technology, organisation and public policy has helped to bring about a sea change in agriculture, food and environment. Foodgrains production has increased four-fold, to support a rapidly increasing population. Per capita income has doubled. There is also an impressive increase in the life expectancy and decline in the infant mortality. Thanks to the cutting edge science and technology. India has moved from the chronic shortages to an era of self-sufficiency in food grains.

The cabinet on 20th March 2001 finally approved the national policy or the empowerment of women. A new scheme on integration of women empowerment project was approved. A distance education programme for women self-help groups was also launched during the year for the holistic development of the child, the department has been implemented the integrated child development services schemes (ICDS) which provides a package of services comprising supplementary nutrition immunisation, health check up and referral services now covers 4384 blocks and is the world's largest and most unique outreach programme for early childhood care.

The department of women and child development continued to recognise the contribution and potential of rich and vibrant civil society organisation, especially the women's groups, all over the country and forged a strong partnership with them for the implementation of many of is innovative schemes and programmes. These organisations also contribute in a big way for the empowerment of women and development of children. Under the schemes of Day Care Centre for Children 12,470 creches provided day care services to children of migrant, casual, agricultural laboureres and construction workers. The Central Social Welfare Board and Indian Council of Child Welfare are implementing the scheme. Under the National Creche Fund, the Department has set up 2455 additional creches.

Early childhood education scheme was started in 1982 to reduce the drop out rates and to improve the rate of retention of children in primary schools. The scheme is being run by voluntary organisations in nine educationally backward States of Andhra Pradesh, Assam, Bihar, Jammu & Kashmir, Madhya Pradesh, Orissa, Rajasthan, Tripura and West Bengal. At present there are 2616 ECE centres in the country integrated with the ICDS network.

Government of India has declared the year 2001 as the year of Women's Empowerment. The Department has finalised a calendar of activities for celebration during every month of the year on themes like, Human Rights for Women, Economic Empowerment of Women, Women and Technology, Women and Governance, Women and Education, Women and Health, Women and Media, Entrepreneurship and Women.

Since the inception of the scheme of Working Women's Hostel, 841 hostels have been sanctioned to provide accommodation to 52,140 working women and day care facilities to 8,012 children in 309 hostels. During the year 20 new hostels were sanctioned. The Cabinet Committee of Economic Affairs has approved the restructuring of Indira Mahila Yojana (IMY) into a Integrated Women's Empowerment Programme (IWEP), and expand it from the existing 238 blocks to 650 blocks by the end of the Ninth plan. The main strategy of the scheme is to create an organisational base for women and to come up together, to analyse and fulfill their needs.

Mass education initiatives through print media for generating awareness and publicity through postal media was also undertaken to inform, educate, and motivate people for bringing about attitudinal changes to receive social education and motivate people for bringing about attitudinal changes to scheme social development goals through electronic and print media are being effectively used to inform, educate and motivate people for bringing about attitudinal of children, women's empowerment, early child development, nutrition, equal status, for women and social civil child marriage, dowry, gender equality, sexual abuses of girl child, exploitation for women and children has been the focus of all media activities. Grant-in-aid to voluntary organisations in the field of women and child to coordinate by the central office to coordinate various activities for women, social awareness sanitation and hygiene and nutrition education with special emphasis on pre school children, dissemination of knowledge of family welfare for innovative programmes in the field of women and child development during the year 2001 is given. The National Film Development Corporation media unit of the department can provide multimedia facilities for which the electronic and print media are being effectively used for different issues concerning women and girl child. Press campaign can also be launched for generating awareness about child labour, nutrition, and infanticide and domestic violence.

Training, Employment and Education

ICAR has also intensified its efforts for transfer of improved technologies by establishing Agriculture Technology Information Centre — a single window delivery system. The functioning of 53 Zonal Research Stations have been emendated at act as Krishi Vigyan Kender in addition to existing 261 kendra, along with the strengthening of institution village linkage programme (IVLP). Under the priority area of crop improvement/ management for various regions and production system has been supported by the generation of the appropriate agro techniques, to provide evolved. The research support to provide training and skill development to women for enhancing their productivity, new upgraded skills to poor and assetless women in additional sector — agriculture, sericulture, fisheries, dairying, poultry etc., for enhancing their producing and income generation.

This programme launched in 1987, seek to provide update skills and new knowledge to poor and assetless women in the traditional sectors, such as, agriculture, animal husbandry, khadi and village industries, sericulture, social forestry and wasteland development of enhancing their productivity and income generation. This would enhance and broaden their employment opportunities, including self-employment and development of entrepreneurial skills. Women beneficiaries are organised into viable and cohesive groups or co-operatives. A comprehensive package of services, such as, extension, inputs, market linkages, etc. are provided besides linkage with credit for transfer of assets.

Women's economic programme, which was launched in 1982-83 with assistance form the Norwegian Agency for Development cooperation. Under this programme, financial assistance is given to women's development corporation, Public Sector Corporation and Voluntary organisations, to train poor women mostly in non-traditional trades and to ensure their employment in these areas. Financial assistance is given to the grantee organisations of hiring of training-cum-production sheds, training costs, machinery and equipment, stipend to the trainees and remuneration for the trainees, the upper ceiling for assistance under this scheme is normally confined to Rs. 8000 per beneficiary.

Distance Education for Women and empowerment and various schemes of the Government, of India have shown that strong women's group could contribute substantially to the development and convergence of services and activities the experience of these schemes has shown that the sustainability of the majority of these groups was a major problem and one of the prime reasons that was lack of proper training strategy. The Department of Women and Child Development, Indira Gandhi National Open University (IGNOU) and Indian Space Research Organisation (ISRO) are jointly undertaking the implementation of the project.

Integrated Child Development Services (ICDS) Scheme

The Integrated Child Development Services (ICDS) Scheme aims to improve the nutritional and health status of pre school children, pregnant women and nursing mothers by providing a package of services including supplementary nutrition, pre school education, health check-up and health education. In addition the scheme envisages effective convergence of inter-sectoral services in the Anganwadi Centres.

Objectives of IDSC

- Improve the nutritional and health status of children below the age of six years.
- Lay the foundation for the proper psychological, physical and social development of the child.
- Reduce the incidence of mortality morbidity malnutrition and school drop-outs.
- Achieve effective coordination of policy and implementation among various departments to promote child development.
- Enhance the capability of the mother to look after the normal health and nutritional needs of the child, through proper health and nutrition education.

The department continued recognise the contribution and the potential of rich and vibrant civil society organisations, specially the women's groups, all over the country and forged a strong partnership with them for the implementation of many of its innovative schemes and programmes. These organisations also contribute in a big way as think tanks, advocates and watchdogs of the development initiatives for the empowerment of women and development of children.

Nutritional Monitoring to be established at state, district, block and community level:

- Community based monitoring mechanism to be established from village level to the level of the state, and responsibility and accountability to be fixed for reduction in malnutrition levels.
- Information on reduction of malnutrition in young children to be reviewed in monthly developmental reviews at district and state levels.
- Database on nutrition situation in the country to be created at the central and state levels and reviewed every quarter by the empowered committee.

Grant-in-aid for Research, Publication and Monitoring

The Department promotes research studies for development of innovative programmes, for testing the feasibility of new proposals, for evaluating the efficacy of existing programmes and services and for analysing emerging problems and services and issues in the field of women and child development. It also supports workshops and seminars which help in formulating research proposals and disseminating research findings of social situational analysis, which are likely to be helpful in planning, programming and review of implementation.

These activities are being carried out through Research

Institutes, Universities, Colleges/Schools of Social Work and Social Organisations. Under the scheme, the organisation should have registered under any state in India and normally have experience for three years in the field of women and child development.

Priority is given to research projects of an applied nature keeping in view factors such as the policy priorities of the department, social problems requiring urgent public interventions and evaluation of the programmes implemented by the department.

Constitutional Provisions

Women and children who represent more than two-third per cent of the country's total population, constitute the most important target groups in the context of developmental planning and therefore, their concerns are placed high on the priority list of the country's developmental agenda.

The concern of safeguarding the rights and privileges of women and children found its best expression in the Constitution of India. While Article 14 confers equal rights and opportunities on men and women in political, economic and social spheres, Article 15 prohibits discrimination against any citizen on the grounds of sex and article 15(3) empowers the State to make affirmative discrimination in favour of women. Article 39 enjoins upon the State to provide equal work and article 42 directs the state to make provisions for ensuring just and humane condones of work and maternity relief. Realising that children have neither a voice nor a political constituency, the Constitution of India and laid down certain social safeguards to ensure their welfare, protection and development. Article 45 provides for free and compulsory education for all children upto age of 14 years.

In order to give a practical shape to the constitutional directives a number of laws have been enacted and schemes and programmes have been formulated for the development of women and children. These have definitely brought forth a perceptible improvement in the status of women and children in the country, although there is still a wide gap between the *de jure* provisions and the *de facto* realities.

Women's Component Plan

The ninth plan directed both the Centre and the States to adopt a special strategy of women's component plan through which, not less than 30 per cent of funds/benefits are earmarked in all the women-related sectors. It also suggested a special vigil to be kept on the flow of the earmarked funds/ benefits through an effective brings forth a holistic approach towards empowering women. The Department of Women and Child Development which was designed as the Nodal Machinery for the development and empowerment of women is playing a crucial role in the formulation and monitoring of women's component plan. The department has advised all the concerned Ministries for inclusion of an identifiable women components plan in their programmes right from the planning process and implementation and monitoring of their programmes to ensure that the benefits of their programmes to reach the women. The committee has been renamed as Committee for Monitoring Gender Mainstreaming in the Government of India.

Special Component Plan (SSP) for SC and Tribal Sub-Plan (TSP) programmes for women and children implemented by the Departments are primarily directed towards the most disadvantaged groups of population like scheduled castes and scheduled tribes and other economically backward classes living in backward rural and tribal areas and urban slums. The basic consideration in all the schemes is to ensure that the benefits of the schemes flow to the disadvantaged sections of the population the SCs and STs, women and children.

Most of the programmes of the department implemented through voluntary organisations. Efforts are made to encourage more and more voluntary organisation to come with proposals in tribal and backward rural areas by special concessions and relaxation under the grant-in-aid. The department at the instance of cabinet secretariat prepares the Annual Action Plan (AAP) for the scheme and activity of the department, setting out the target fixed at the beginning of the year.

Agricultural Research of India's ninth five year plan (1997-2002) DARE requested with the endorsement of parliamentary standing committee on agriculture, for allocation of 1 per cent of AGDP for public expenditure on agricultural research, extension education. From previous precedent, plan allocations usually fall some twenty-five per cent short of requests. They nevertheless customarily exceed funding available from domestic sources incorporating an assumed contribution from external financing to cover the projected gap. These have been steady growth in ICAR, SAU & ZRS infrastructure and staff employed. The system now serves almost all of India agro-climatic zones yet despite of this build up there have been a number of funding problems.

Production practices and systems will need to be adopted to respond to new market demands and export opportunities, poverty alleviation or growing labour shortage, depending on the setting. Technical solutions will be increasingly location specific, matched to the huge diversity of India's 20 agro ecological regions, 60 sub-regions and 120 agro-climatic zones. More detailed indigenous knowledge and greater skills in blending modern and traditional technologies to optimise productive efficiency will be more than even before — the keys to farming success and sectoral growth. And while ready-made intensification technology may be importable for a few commercial and particularly export producer, most of the needed technology will still have to be generated and adapted locally to make it compatible with the social and economic circumstances of Indian farmers. Much of the adopted technology will therefore remain into the category of public goods. Finally it will be necessary to address growing environmental concerns, especially natural resources conservation. These include the needs for better conservation of the land and water base of irrigated agriculture, a reduction of agro climatic pollution and adverse health effects, production of fragile ecosystems in mountain, coastal and arid areas and the containment of deforestation by traditional shifting cultivation.

Mechanisms needed simply to improve timely communication would be very different from those required to launch an integrated research and extension programme. Similarly, the mechanisms needed to develop collaboration between two groups that resent losing their autonomy will differ markedly from those needed to link groups that recognise their interdependence but simply do not set enough time to work together and share information. The basic types of linkage mechanisms. These mechanisms apply to link between on-station and on-farm research as well as between research and technology transfer agencies. Many of these mechanisms can also be used to forge link directly with the farmers. The specific to highlight each mechanisms' particular utility for building links, its management requirements, and the kind of institutional conditions under which it can be used most effectively through planning and review process. The mechanisms also functions best when managers set them up to advisor, with professional pooling their respective area of expertise, rather than supervisory with one group acting as watch dog over the other for joint problem diagnosis; joint priority setting; and planning exercise joint programming and review meetings.

Indian agriculture must also capture some more opportunities. The biological revolution has provided the precedent opportunity of transforming any gene from any organism and is already having an impact on agricultural development in several developed, and a few developing countries.

Contribution of technology generation, assessment, refinement and transfer to sector growth. If it is to respond successfully to these challenges, agriculture will have to become more knowledge intensive investments in research will be needed to generate new knowledge. Greater attention will have to be paid to information based technologies. Strengthened means of dissemination will be needed to transfer will have to focus more strongly than before the keys to farming success and sectoral growth. And while ready-made intensification technology may be importable for a few commercials and particularly export producers, most of the needed to generate the new knowledge. Greater attention will have to be paid to information-based technologies strengthened means of dissemination will be needed to transmit this information to farmers since vast majority will still have to hectares or use of garble land, or correspondingly small livestock to enterprises, there they will continue to be strict limits on the amounts of cost recovery which they can support; much of the adopted technology will therefore remain in the category of public goods. Finally it has been necessary to address growing environmental concerns, especially natural resource conservation. These for better conservation of land and water base of irrigated agriculture and reduction of agro chemical pollution and adverse health effects protection of fragile ecosystems in mountain coastal arid areas and the contaminant of deforestation by traditional shift cultivation to capture some novel opportunities.

Contribution of technology generation assessment, refinement. If it is respond successfully to these challenges agriculture will have to become more knowledge intensive in the management by the producers of their available resources, sustainability, coping with diversity by adapting technology more specifically to agro-ecological or social circumstances, and raising the economic efficiency of agriculture. To make information transfer more cost effective, greater use will need to be made of modern information technology in communication between researchers, extensionists and their fanner clients. The techniques of frontier sciences of intense biotechnology will have to be further developed.

Biodiversity and Environment

Projects may vary from research involving extensive fieldwork or social surveys based on thosé of a more theoretical nature. The aim is to produce a written thesis which is a sustained argument based on a thorough review of evidence and critical inquiry offering original insights at a theoretical or empirical level for life on earth. The ground breaking reports shall indicate the profound changes that continue to occur in social, institutional and economic systems. The students are required to undertake taught courses in research methods drawn from the M.Sc. research methods in social science during the first year of M.Phil, and Ph.D. studies. Other courses from across the university may be taken if they are relevant to the student research.

A main supervisor shall be appointed when the student arrives at the school/centre and within a few months other people may be appointed as appropriate and in consultation with the student. Supervisors appointed provide advice on all aspects of the form and content of research, and the research process, and ensure that students meet the universities various quality control requirements. Undertaking research and producing a thesis can be a long process and supervisors are also important in helping to keep students motivated.

Entry Requirement

Successful research relies a great deal on motivation, considerable personal commitment is vital. Research students generally have ethic a good honours degree, a master degree or relevant professional experience. The required standard increases substantially from B.Phil, to Ph.D. they must also research interest which match those of potential supervisors.

Acceptance is based on formal application from and interview. Applicants are expected to have prepared an outline research proposal at the point of application.

Finding

Significant progress has been made in confronting environmental challenges. Nevertheless, the environment has continued to degrade in nations of all regions. Progress towards a sustainable future has simply been too slow.

A regional and participatory process was used to produce analysis of environmental impact of alternative development scenarios and policy action will be included in the further GEO report as well as more extensive analysis of current policy responses, their impact, and the reasons for their success and failures. The introduction of these elements in the continuous GEO assessment has already started. As a result several countries report marked progress in curbing environment pollution and showing the rate of resource degradation as well as reducing the intensity of resource use.

International Agenda in 1992 in Rio de Janeiro provides the global consensus on the road map towards sustainable development. UNEP continues to be the environmental voice of United Nations responsible development, scientific analysis monitoring and assessment. Increasingly, United Nation Organisations, the World Bank and regional banks are "greening" their programme. New approaches to international policies are being developed, tested and implemented.

Collaborative arrangements: with the network of institutions on JNU campus like Institute of Mass Communication the Indian Council of Social Science Research Campus will substantially promote networking amongst scientists and cater to each other needs.

The ninth plan directed both the center and the states to adopt a special strategy of women's component plan through which, not less than 30 per cent of funds/ benefits are earmarked in all the women-related sectors. It also suggested a special vigil to be kept on the flow of the earmarked funds / benefits through an effective brings forth a holistic approach towards empowering women. The Department of Women and Child Development which was designed as the Nodal Machinery for the development and empowerment of women is playing a crucial role in the formulation and monitoring of women's component plan. The department has advised all the concerned Ministries for inclusion of an identifiable women components plan in their programs right from the planning process and implementation and monitoring of their programs to ensure mat the benefits of their programs to ensure that the benefits reach the women. The committee has been renamed as Committee for Monitoring Gender Mainstreaming in the Government of India.

Special component Plan (SCP) for SC and Tribal Sub-Plan (TSP) programs for women and children implemented by the Departments are primarily directed towards the most disadvantaged groups of population like scheduled casts and scheduled tribes and other economically backward classes living in backward rural and tribal areas and urban slums. The basic consideration in all the schemes is to ensure hat he benefits of the schemes flow to the disadvantaged sections of the population the SCs and STs, women and children.

Most of the programs of the departmental implemented through voluntary organizations. Efforts are made to encourage more and more voluntary organization to come with proposals in tribal and backward rural areas by special concessions and relaxation under the grant-in-aid. The department at the instance of cabinet secretariat prepares the annual action plan (AAP) for the scheme ad activity o the department, setting out the target fixed at the beginning of the year.

Agricultural Research of India's ninth five year plan (1997-

2002) DARE requested with the endorsement of parliamentary standing committee on agriculture, for allocation of 1 per cent of AGDP for public expenditure on agricultural research, extension education. From previous precedent, plan allocations usually fall some twenty five percent short of requests. They nevertheless customarily exceed funding available from domestic sources incorporating an assumed contribution from external financing to cover the projected gap. These have been steady growth in ICAR. SAU & ZRS infrastructure and staff employed. The system now serves almost all of India agro-climatic zones yet despite of this build up there have been a number of funding problems.

Production practices and systems will need to be adopted to respond to new market demands and export opportunities, poverty alleviation or growing labour shortage, depending on the setting. Technical solutions will be increasingly location specific, matched to the huge diversity of India's 20 agro ecological regions, 60 sub-regions and 120 agro-climatic zones. More detailed indigenous knowledge and greater skills in blending modern and traditional technologies to optimize productive efficiency will be more than even before-the keys to farming success and sectoral growth. And while ready-made intensification technology may be importable for a few commercial and particularly export producer, most of the needed technology will still have to be generated and adapted locally to make it compatible with the social and economic circumstances of Indian farmers. Since the vast majority will still have two hectares or less of arable land, or less of arable land, or correspondingly small live stock enterprises, there will continue to be strut limits on the amount of cost recovery, which they can support. Much of the adopted technology will therefore remain into he category of public goods. Finally it will be necessary to address growing environmental concerns, especially natural resources conservation. These include the needs for better conservation of the land and water base of irrigated agriculture, a reduction of agro climatic pollution and adverse health effects, production of fragile ecosystems in mountain, coastal and arid areas and the containment of mountain, coastal and arid areas and the containment of deforestation by traditional shifting cultivation.

Mechanisms needed simply to improve timely communication would be very different from those required to launch an integrated research and extension program. Similarly, the mechanisms needed to develop collaboration between two groups that resent losing their autonomy will differ markedly from those needed to link groups that recognize their interdependence but simply do not set enough time to work together and share information.

The basic types of linkage mechanisms. These mechanisms apply to link between on station and on-farm research as well as between research and technology transfer agencies. Many of these mechanisms can also be used to forge link directly with the farmers The specific to highlight each mechanisms' particular utility for building links, its management requirements, and the kind of institutional conditions under which it can be used most effectively through planning and review process The mechanisms also functions best when managers set them up to advisor, with professional pooling their respective area of expertise, rather than supervisory with one group acting as watch dog over the other for joint problem diagnosis; joint priority setting; and planning exercise joint programming and review meetings.

Indian agriculture must also capture some more opportunities. The biological revolution has provided the precedent opportunity of transforming any gene from any organism and is already having an impact on agricultural development in several developed, and a few developing countries.

Contribution of technology generation, Assessment, refinement and transfer to sector growth: If it is to respond successfully to these challenges, agriculture will have to become more knowledge intensive investments in research will be needed to generate new knowledge. Greater attention will have to be paid to information based technologies. Strengthened means of dissemination will be needed to transfer will have to focus more strongly than before the keys to farming success and sectoral growth. And while ready-made intensification technology may be importable for a few commercials and particularly export producers, most of the needed to generate the new knowledge. Greater attention will have to be paid to information-based technologies strengthened means of dissemination will be needed to transmit this information to fanners Since vast majority will still have to hectares or use of garble land, or correspondingly small live stock to enterprises, there they will continue to be strict limits on the amounts of cost recovery which they can support; much of the adopted technology will therefore remain in the category of public goods. Finally it has been necessary to address growing environmental concerns, especially natural resource conservation. These for better conservation of land and water base of irrigated agriculture and reduction of agro chemical pollution and adverse health effects protection of fragile Eco-systems in mountain coastal arid areas and the contaminant of deforestation by traditional shift cultivation to capture some novel opportunities.

Programmes

- MA Multidisciplinary Programme
- MSc Research Methods in Social Science
- MA Criminology
- MA Social Policy
- MSc Psychology and Health
- MA/Pg Dip Social Work
- MA Social Work 'Top Up'
- Employment Route MA/PG Dip. Social Work

- MA Psychoanalysis
- MA/MSc Sustainable Environmental Management
- (Geography and Environment Management)
- (Water Management)
- MA Local Economic Development
- MA Sustainable Rural Development
- MSc In Arboriculture and Community Forest Management
- PG Dip/MA/MSc Inter professional Healthcare
- MSc/PG Dip Mental Health Interventions

Graduate Studies in the Field of Social Sciences

Aft interdisciplinary approach, particularly with regard to studies of environmental issues, gender, reach ethnicity, is a significant feature. Particular attention is given to the theory and development of advance research methods and acquisition of key skills for the conduct of upto date and innovative research practice.

The post graduate community which provides its members with support and simulation. Academic staff facilitates the learning in a variety of ways. Academic staff involved in postgraduate work is active in research and producing publication

The Post Graduate programs are always being update in the line with changing knowledge and demand. For work experience internship modules which can take place of one to two taught options for a taught maser degree academic year 1996-1997 on wards. There were 214 universities and deemed universities including 27 agricultural universities, 2 veterinary universities, 4 medical universities and 2 technological universities with the affiliated colleges constituting the target segment of the higher institutions of higher education, the total teaching staff in the universities and affiliated colleges was 3.21 lakhs as against 3.10 lakhs in the previous year.

We are a country of rich heritage. Our culture accorded a high position to women in society. It is unfortunate that over the years the very security that was built for women became a barrier for their advancement and deprived them of education and confined them to home. We now have the opportunity to show the world how this trend can be reversed and women accorded an equal status with men.

NODAL CENTRE FOR HUMAN ECOLOGY

Financial Mechanism

For the projects-for the development of infrastructure for:

- Relevance of education
- Promoting of excellence and quality in education
- Equity and access for management of higher education and UGC administration for "Financial Mechanism"

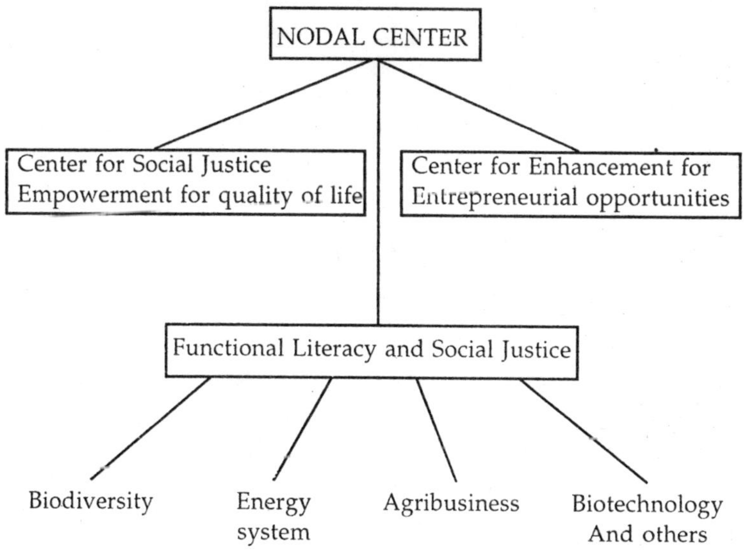

Education develops man power for different levels of economy and empowers the poor masses to become self-reliant enough to participate in the process of nation development.

The main objectives of the proposed center will be:

- To identify various target groups of human ecology for women as well as those who are to be trained in imparting and in developing the field of human ecology and consequent.
- To review currently employed teaching methods and assess how far these are suitable, and what appropriate methods and training programmes need to be devised.

CHAPTER 3

COMMUNITY EMPOWERMENT

Empowerment to Women

The progression of women from their present status of real empowerment is a very dynamic process and there are many milestones to be crossed before the same is reached. The state government is committed to create an enabling environment in which women in all strata of society particularly rural women can actualize their potential. Already there is a significant movement in the shape of self help groups for women particularly DWCRA groups who are participating not only income generating activities, but social issues also.

The tribal situation to put it mildly, is explosive. The North-Eastern region continues to be the cause of anxiety. We are passing through a regime of economic reforms. Women in transition economic are finding that their specific skills are becoming obsolete. In the tribal societies women play a major role especially in economic field. In spite of the development taking place all round, it has to be conceded that bulk of the tribal women will continue to live and earn livehood in their own environment. We should also not lose sight of the fact that the majority of tribal women will continue to be engaged in traditional agricultural and forest sectors. It is therefore, appropriate that attention should be focused more and more on these sectors and on prospects and opportunities arising therefrom. Science and technology has to play a significant role in these fields in improving the status of tribal women.

Although women are given reservation, they to face many problems because of remote area, illiteracy the rate of rural women literacy being approximately 80 per cent. They are also hesitant to participate in public activities because there is an age-old tradition of man recognized as the bread winner and women doing household work. As such her participation in public life has been minimal. Here lies the challenge for women, the social workers, NGOs, the State commission and the National Commission, We have to boost the moral of women to reiterate that we are also equally capable of doing public administration, equally capable of managing the affairs of the village as we can manage the affairs of our house: Such morale boosting is very necessary because women cannot have the confidence to act an effective member.

In the recent years, the problem of rehabilitation of certain maladjusted groups in society has become important. This is reflected in the fact that the Government have started taking an interest in this field and promulgated a number of acts for the furtherance of preventive measures in respect of immoral traffic in women, juvenile delinquents, beggars, etc. Steps have been taken also to set up reduce home, schools, probation hostels and other institutions.

In the circumstances, training in the field of correctional work assumes special importance. There is a growing realization in the country that the work of reclaiming and reforming criminals and of dealing with maladjusted individuals and groups can be done more effectively by trained social workers. Habitual offenders, fallen women, juvenile delinquents, beggars, criminal tribes, all these have to be treated with sympathy and understanding. For the proper study of criminal problems, it is necessary to train specialists in many areas such as anthropology, sociology, law, education, etc. It is, therefore, encouraging to find some schools of social work taking an interest in the subject.

Family and Child Care

We look upon the child today as a pivot of the family and the hope of the future. But human history has a different tale to tell. In the early history of humanity marked by an acute struggle for existence, infanticide was quite common and it has lingered on even in our times in backward communities. The art of bringing up the child was left to nature. The child was often looked upon as an economic asset in agriculture, so that even parents did not accept his right to education. Compulsory education was barely in existence even in the most advanced countries till just a century ago. But it was left to the famous Swedish feminist Ellen Key to look upon the 20th century as the century of the child. Today the right of the child to be educated and to play, to enjoy good health and to grow up to a healthy manhood is universally accepted. It is in his interest that antenatal care has come into being and post-natal care is looked upon as an absolute desideratum. Thus the importance of the family as the very basis of society has come to be recognized. It can once be seen that family and child welfare represent an important field of social work.

Work of the Aged

The need of dealing with the old is not so acute in India as in the West where remarkable homes for the aged have sprung up. In India the joint family still survives, though it has crumbled in urban areas, but even here the old family have still lingers and the aged are generally looked after by their children Unfortunately there are families where the individualism of the West has corroded family life and the neglect of the old has not been uncommon. The time is not too far off when the problem of the old will become more acute and is bound to figure as an important field of social work.

Welfare of the Handicapped

The welfare of the handicapped involves considerable expenditure, but the government with its restricted resources is willing to do what it can, for help to the handicapped has been the legacy of India from ancient times. Now that the rehabilitation of the handicapped has become possible, Government cannot shirk the duty of doing what it can for those that need most to be assisted.

Thus welfare services would include looking after the socially maladjusted like the beggars, prostitutes, delinquents and physically or mentally handicapped. The huge population of normal people, most of whom are oppressed by poverty, constitutes an enormous problem by itself.

With the policies adopted by the government, it is clear that there is a great need for trained social workers and hence there is ample room for schools of social work. Social workers' education has to be organized to fulfil the needs of the various types of social work required. If the social policies of the government are to succeed, it can not do so through the efficient and devoted services of the trained social workers.

The need for trained social workers is, however, paramount in the present situation. This implies a network of efficient social work schools. The main business of the committee appointed by the UGC and the Ministry of Eduction was to focus their attention on the quality of training imparted in these institutions. We hope the recommendations would receive serious attention from the institutions concerned after they have been duly considered by the UGC and the Ministry of Education.

Social Justice

University Grants Commission plans to be a major national partner in the promotion of human rights culture and considers it to be one of the major objectives of higher education.

However, it is essential to consider the specific national environment of the user and to adapt training material to local situation to ensure their suitability in different context. The kinds of issues which were undertaken on the inaugural Verma speech on the empowerment of women Verma of Justice Verma into account include: a national legislation and policy on women, the social status and juridical practices relating to women worker's rights, the discriminatory aspects in gender relations at the national level; and the existing level of legal literacy among women worker, women organization and community at large.

EDUCATION EXTENSION AND OUTREACH

Education for HRD

The Concept

The managerial term highly talked about little understood and yet somewhat less practised today in India is Human Resource Development. Although the term began to be used in the Indian corporate circle in the early 70s, it gained popularity in the country only when the Government of India constituted the Ministry of Human Resource Development at the centre. It was realized, for the first time, both at the macro and micro operations that the development of the country or organization depended to a greater extent on the development of human resource of different types rather than the development of material resources such as the land and building, capital machine, material, technology, etc., and that the integration of the group goals with the national goals and employees; goals with the organizational goals essential ingredients for overall growth and development. Since then, several organizations belonging to the private, public and joint sectors of the country have either started new HRD departments or appointed HRD managers or taken initiative to strengthen their personnel departments to look after the HRD functions. In nutshell, the HRD movement has taken off in the country.

Present Scenario

The HRD movement, which began in the country during the 80s of the current century, has remained lop-sided, that is, confined to the managerial personnel only even after the lapse of more than 25 years. The HRD of workers is deliberately overlooked. Advancing on the traditional path of Marxism, the trade union organizations of the country have remained passive and mostly slient on the unions' role in educating the workers of HRD. The subjects covers, so far, under the grants-in-aid programs to trade unions/other institutions of the Central Board of Workers' Education are mostly legal or economic and not developmental. The reason for the total apathy of the trade union leaders towards workers' education for HRD is, perhaps, the fear that their leadership may be in danger if a new class of contented, satisfied, self-dependent and assertive workers looking after their own interests emerges out of the HRD-oriented educational programs. The workers may even ask for their participation in the union affairs and this will not be in the interest of the ageing and retired trade union activities heading the Trade Union Movement of the country. Moreover, these trade union leaders do not want to assume the collaborative role and want to confine with the traditional roles as this practice may reduce their bargaining power and shift the workers' loyality from unions to managements. The relegation of workers affairs to the corporate Industrial Relations Department having no coordination with the HRD Department shows the aversion of the corporate managements towards the HRD education for workers. The effects of any educational and developmental efforts directed on a particular group of employees and overlooking altogether the rank and file comprising the majority of the total human assets of any organization are bound to be marginal and halfhearted from the viewpoint of organizational growth and development and as such, undesirable.

Restructuring and Productivity

The world is in transition from the industry-based and regional or national based society of 19-20th century to a knowledge-based and 'one world one village' or global society in the 21st century. This is the advent of the information technology era that is due to the convergence of the computer, communication and electronic technologies. In the 21st century, knowledge will be the key and the fundamental sources of wealth will be knowledge and information rather than raw materials and labour.

It is particularly strong in four leading sectors: information and communication technologies, intellectual property-patents, brand names, advertising and financial services: databases and recreational services; and biotechnology. It is often said if we can transport lots of bits so easily and so quickly and so economically, there is no need to transport raw materials and physical labour.

The mantra of getting competitive edge in the age of liberalization and globalization is Lead of Follow. Therefore, going for 'lead' is the best mantra of the present days' competitive advantages. Poor countries like India, have thus to go for a 'lead' through improved human resources generation in a process of evolution, which shall be innovative and rapid. Till today, human generation is not done at factory but at the institutions of higher learning and research like universities, engineering and medical colleges/institutes, etc. The speculation of 'self-designing beings' who would continue to improve themselves at an ever increasing rate. Under such situations, the reduced budget allocation for higher education, implemented in recent past in many poor countries is not beyond the preview of questions and criticism.

The Case of India

Since 1992, India has taken part in the liberalization, privatization and globalization process. So India needs to improve human resources particularly in technical/higher education and research. But in international standing of higher education and research, not only India's position is poor but also it is becoming poorer day by day. Irony is that this picture has emerged after India's taking part in liberalization process, whereas this should have been be the other way round. There are different parameters to see the position of human resources, like Human Resources Index defined by the UNO, etc. For the purpose of higher education and research, we may analyze data based on other more appropriate parameters..

It is amply clear that India is not following the correct path to become a leader in the world of globalization In poor countries and, therefore, in India also, it is often assumed that higher education is not appropriate at the cost of other social infrastructure like basic education, health, etc. But we must analyze whether higher education is really costly in India, and if so what are the reasons for that and must find path to abnegate those reasons. Higher education in India is costly because of the following reasons:

1. India, and for that matter most or all of the poor countries' education system and structure are copied or borrowed from advanced countries. We have no innovative system and structure of our own to meet our environment and requirements.
2. Investment return on higher education in poor countries including India is low.
3. Imbalance and improper fund allocation to the institutes.

Fare and Share

In the present day pattern of education, all the students admitted in any course have to undergo study for a fixed period of time, irrespective of student's ability. Even if a students is able to learn all about the course in a shorter period he is not supposed to do so. Similarly, a less meritorious student is hard pressed by the system itself to complete the course during the fixed time. To overcome the problem and to make our technical education appropriate to the globalization process that needs fast learning, we suggest that for the courses of B.Tech/B.E. *Fare* is for "learn fast' jargon. Nowadays the students of NRI category and others on capitation fees being admitted in technical education, hardly considering the merit. *Share,* therefore, may be an actual requirement.

Investment Return on Higher Education

It is often said that the investment return on higher education is less or marginal. The marginal rates for the college and university in India are lower that the returns for below college level studies. Therefore, more investments and higher subsidies on the education below college level would be more beneficial for both the individual and the society than that on higher education. But in this study only individual income was considered for the calculation of return. In case of higher education more emphasis should be given to the national income than the individual income. For example, an engineer's monthly salary is not the only return, his service in terms of production in the factory, development of techniques and system (that may be assumed as income of nation through his service) are the major returns.

The main reasons for low investment return on higher education are (a) brain drain, and (2) non-involvement of professional persons in the policy framing of even project specific matters.

The gravity of the problem caused by brain-drain shall minimize if people migrating abroad shall even marginally invest in nation building. Nowadays, NRIs are participating in the national projects and developments. This is encouraging at the same time, we do something atleast to reduce. Higher perks and pay and freedom in work place of progressional persons are the major issues need to be considered seriously to reduce brain-drain.

Any move to limit higher education and research by any means shall be counterproductive for growth and prosperity of the nation. The argument that poor countries should not and cannot bear the high cost of higher education, and that too at the expenses of elementary education and basic health, etc., is good to hear in the first instance.

Criteria for distribution of funds to the institutes of higher learning and research by a parameter of productivity of the institutes rather than their products and image, etc., has also been proposed. It is believed that suggestions made in here in conformity with the tenet 'think globally act locally' which is often taken as the way of going with liberalization. Reducing higher education in poor countries shall be first suicidal step in the age of open economy and information revolution.

The proper analysis of this argument and whether higher eduction is really costly and if so what are the reasons behind that need to be examined before taking a decision.

The Nineth Plan Guidelines and Approach

Following are the main thrust in the Nineth Plan guidelines of UGC for centres/ departments of Adult Continuing Education and Extension and field outreach:

1. In the Nineth plan, every university should establish a centre/department of Adult Continuing Education and Extension. The adult continuing education and outreach activities should become an integral part of all departments and constituents of the university through the optimum involvement of teachers and students. The universities need to give a statutory status to the departments/centres for Adult Continuing Education and Extension, if needed even by amending the University Acts and

Statutes. The department/centre will have the same status as any other academic/ teaching department of the university with core faculty eligible for representation on all the university bodies such as senate, academic council, board of studies, etc.

Adult Continuing Education and Extension during the Nineth Plan are the following:

Undergraduate and postgraduate level courses in adult and continuing education/non-formal education

Certificate/diploma courses in adult education

Projects related to extension/field outreach and foundation courses

Research/Documentation/Publication. Training programs for students/ community/teachers

Vocational/career-oriented programs empowering people at different socio-economic and educational levels with marketable vocational skills and to provide an opportunity to update skill or acquire a qualification for career advancement.

Quality of life improvement programs for upgrading living standards

Leadership and human resource development

Social and citizenship role awareness

Individual interest program for promoting personal development.

HUMAN ECOLOGY-UPDATING THE CURRICULA WITH SPECIAL REFERENCE TO HOME SCIENCE

Home science, in reality is deeply and closely related to life, being so close it may often look common place and ordinary in general parlance of human affairs. A model home science curriculum would, therefore, care to cover all such factors, fields and interests which effect a person's development, his life, in the family and in the community, under the world of work. That is, home science course ought be vitally effect improvement in living conditions on the basis of scientific understanding of environment and the use of scientific methods in solving daily life problems. Thus various aspect of home science enumerated above need to be interwoven and integrated in the curriculum at school level in the following pattern; which would call for an urgent attention of curriculum framers and planners to give its due while restructuring curriculum in new pattern. This would also need careful sifting of the home science content and practical work expected of children at different stages and streams of education.

Home Science education in its variety of forms possesses a very high deal of potentialities for contributing to the world of work and can provide employment opportunity to large number of people. Home Science in its modern context is not nearly restricted to home making or improvement in the prospects of girl's marriage; it is on the contrary an immensely broad based discipline full of rich academic, vocational and profession elements which need to be exploited to the fullest extent in future educational needs of our citizens.

Professional orientation to curriculum, enhancing professionals for making graduates self reliant, the professional courses would provide wider specturm of experience to graduating students hence sufficient weightage have to be given to make students professions and befitted in development departments. The discipline of home science is one such innovation which educates and trains individuals to face with vigour and confidence the challenges of society for self and family, scientifically and technically in the most befitting ways. This discipline has its existence since last fifty years. Now it is peak time to synchronize owe work plan with priorities.

What is the contribution of home science to the society such as industry, firms, institution and services related to employment provided by home science?

How the effects of new curricula will affect the employment profile and economic elevation of the community?

How human resources would be better utilized?

How this change would help compare home science education at par with other countries and globally?

In conclusion we ought to be sensitive to the evolutionary changes that are taking place irrespective of this discipline. We have to be risk taking and innovative in view of the dynamic changes of global liberalization and marketing strategies.

Transformation from Home Science to Human Ecology

The colleges of home science can undergo a change to meet the challenges and opportunities of todays higher education enterprise. Faculty and administrators of the college can be highly motivated for active involvement in planning and self-study initiatives on course of renewal. These initiatives can provide many opportunities for us to engage in stimulating and productive dialogue that can lead in transformative problem-solving and decision-making strategies.

The strategies can be implemented with the recognition that our learning environment must operate within the context of higher education call for greater effectiveness, efficiency and accountability. The basic principle of action and renewal is to retain and improve on teaching, research and outreach programs that are successful and to replace those that are no longer relevant.

Transformative directions for the new millennium reflects the careful and informative thinking and rethinking. It is the synthesis of the outcomes of both individual units initiatives and college level initiatives. The result of our collaborative process with national and international home science education systems can integrate and provide a holistic perspective of home science colleges. These programs herein should not be viewed as a static. They will undergo important transformations that are relevant to the demands of our global society and will improve the human condition of individuals and families within the context of their communities.

Outreach

Home Science Extension

Home science extension was introduced in the colleges and agricultural universities after launching of the community development program in 1952. This was due to the realization of the fact that women can contribute to the natural economy authority to the natural development. Therefore, home science colleges being exclusively for women in those days, took up the task of training their students for extending knowledge of home science.

Recently there has been move in areas of home science to include a component of extension service in their curriculum. It is called home science education, which aims at further developing the capacity of girls and women mainly involved in farm and home making activities. Thus home science extension means the type of education which is extended beyond the four walls of classroom to those who have been deprived of formal education in home science for some reasons.

The term home science extension as the dimension of social science which concerns itself with functional and attitudinal changes in the home and the family through scientific and technological knowledge.

Home science extension deals with the means-methodology of dissemination of scientific and technical information in the area of home science to the people to whom scientific and technical information is of significance in their activities, production and improvement.

The concept of home science extension has to be treated as multidimensional and interdisciplinary since it involves various aspects such as technology, growth and investment opportunities for women, building up the capacity of women, their roles and responsibilities, etc. Home science extension is applied science which aims at bring up about change in behaviour of the target groups through dissemination of scientific and technical information in the area of home science. The important component of home science are: extension education, extension service and extension work.

Home science extension is concerned with teaching research and extension which are the functions of the universities, and institutions of research, extension and higher learning. It is need based programme which adopts a problem solving approach and utilize locally available resource.

Vision

Providing leadership in preparing global minded professionals to meet the society relevant challenges and opportunities of the future.

Mission

Strengthening and empowering individuals and families to interact effectively with their environments.

Values

Dynamic ecological and global prospectives of people, contexts and events Knowledge that improves daily lives of current and future generations

Creativity and critical thinking.

Access to information, education and technology

Collaborations

Excellence, integrity and professionalism

Building on strengths of students and programs

Diversity of people and ideas.

Proposed Schedule of Courses for One Year Postgraduate Diploma in Human Ecology

Module 1	Module II	Module 111	Module IV
Agriculture and Environment	Extension education and Management	Farming system-practices	Legal Environment
Nutrition and health related issues	Rural sociology	Production and operation management	Agribusiness, Post-harvest and processing. Biotechnology
Women and Development	Communication and Audio Visual for Development	Financial management Managerial	Biodiversity and environment Non-conventional energy systems
Computer basic	Management and Extension	Management of formal and non-formal enterprise	Optionals on Farm, off farm. Non-farm sections Creche Religion
July 1 5th-Sept. 25th	Oct. Ist-Dec31st	Jan. 10th-March March 15th-April 15	April 16th-June

Duration of the course — One year
Working hours — 5 days a week with 8 hours per day

Total Maximum marks 1000 Module I — (4 written papers — 200 + Practical—50)
Module II — —do—
Module III — —do—
Module IV — (Written paper— 50 + Project work—200 marks)

For each written paper of 50 marks — 45 hrs of teaching
For each practical paper of 50 marks — 45 hrs of laboratory work

Points of Distinction

Opportunities for the degree programmes to prepare them 'adequately or very well for their employment

A unique multidisciplinary approach integrating outreach and research

Basic and applied research addressing society relevant problems such as child care, welfare reform, diet and career, and universal design, etc.,

Dietetics and nutrition programs in collaboration with national and international peers and organizations

Programs expanding opportunities for study abroad and involvement in international research and outreach initiatives

A community service master degree program for professional development and service including military personnel and dependents.

A child development and teaching program with a new concentration in language arts, child development departments, laboratories of early childhood programs.

Innovative child development educational exchange program for foreign students

Innovations in the Discovery of Knowledge

For continuous evaluation, selection and application of best technology available in support of vision and mission and in pursuit of excellence

To understand the importance of creating the best learning environment and how those can change—from day to day, student to student, and place to place.

To understand the importance of integrating technology into a dynamic learning environment.

To learn the appropriate use of state-of-the-art technology as tool for facing the complex problems of individuals families and communities, of education, business, industry and government.

Multimedia technology for the discovery of knowledge content: Computer laboratories, Computer assisted instruction, Computer aided design (CAD) instruction, Distance—learning technologies, Certificate courses for working professionals, Teleconferences for lifelong learning, Internet-based Virtual university' Instruction, Experimental learning in business, government, industry and community organizations, and Model community-university collaborations. Seminars and lectures by renowned experts and visionaries.

Global Perspectives

Human ecological perspective is global in its approach and provides leadership in international programming at International Centre for Human Ecology and to offer many opportunities for faculty and students to participate in research and study around the world including. International exchanges. Study abroad, Visiting scholars, and Faculty scholarship and research.

Outreach and service: Bringing research and knowledge to our communities. The factors related to early success among children born to teenage mothers project supports parents, their children and families with strategics for better beginnings and successful outcomes.

The community Gang Violence Research Project focuses on community based strategies for addressing gang violence.

The community school project integrates home and school environments to increase students' achievement.

The family and child clinic reaches out to the local community with marital and family therapy services.

The ethnic families projects focus on the strengths of families with mentally retarded and learning disabled children research with a public health perspective.

Public policy and community action for working parents and their children. Food safety and Toxicology initiatives work from farm to help ensure a safe and healthy food supply.

Research for a New Century

Enhancement the potential of children, youth and families optimizing economic change and development

Designing environments for quality of life

Improving nutrition and health

Partnerships

Career Options

Management Specialities

- The field of education
- Social welfare particularly related to women and children
- Human Resources Development

These specialists can work in following organizations

(a)Government: Ministries of HRD, Social Empowerment, Women and Child Welfare

(b)Non-Government: Working for the disadvantaged sections, the poor, the illiterate, the slum women, the street children as well as the aged

(c)International: UNICEF, UNESCO, UNCHR, UNFPA, FAO and other related agencies

Researchers

- Agro based, food processing
- Designing of suitable work places based on agronomics as well as suitable equipment

- Socio-economic dynamic of introduction and acceptance of new technologies
- Need assessment of specific target groups for improving the productivity at home and place of work.

Communication Specialities in the Mass Communication Industry

- Designing of communication aids like posters, etc.
- Designing and implementation of communication campaign for special target groups.
- Designing for different mass media with special reference to electronic, Audiovisual production, print media, etc.
- Developing resource material for different programs like immunization, adult education, etc.

Teachers, Lecturers, Professors in School and Colleges
Women Counsellors

- For individual as well as consumer groups and organization.
- For sensitizing the consumer towards their right, responsibilities as well as means available for conservation protection.
- For working as active members of regional and apex bodies formed by Government in order to protect the interest of concern.

Women Entrepreneurs

- Handicrafts, cottage and small scale industries
- Food preservation and processing industries
- Catering at commercial level
- Interior decorators
- Dairy industries, etc.

Extension Officers

- Health and nutrition
- Agriculture and dairy
- Adult education
- Social empowerment
- Making concrete efforts towards elimination of gender bias and other social evils
- Uplifting their status within the family community and society
- Thus leading to a better quality of life for themselves as well as family members

Home Managers by Empowering Women with

- Better planning, organization and controlling abilities
- Upgrading skill of women in different fields
- Improving their productivity
- Development of desirable values and attitudes
- Giving recognition to productive role played by women and increasing their visibility in work.

Higher Education

1. Masters in extension education
2. Masters in community resource management
3. Masters in education
4. Masters and diploma in mass communication and advertising
5. Masters in management specialization
6. Masters in social work
7. Masters in mass communication with focus on electronic media, programs production, TV film, Radio Audio-visual production slides with sound
8. Masters in aromatic and medicinal plants

9. Masters in Food Sciences and Human Nutrition
10. Masters in Biodiversity conservation and environment on bioremediation, waste treatment and conversion to useful products
11. Masters in Medical Biotechnology—AIDS, Tuberculosis, Typhoid.˙Leishmaniasis, Paralysis, Malaria, Amoebiasis, Cholera, Rabies, Development of vaccines, Oncology, Transgenics, Drug delivery Systems, Genetic Clinic cum Counselling
12. Masters in Industrial Biotechnology, Microbial production of plant growth. Food Biotechnology, Culture and Cultivation of Seawed For food. Development of process for flavours and food additives, Microbial bio-transformation to telpenes of high valued food flavours, Biotechnology research for food safety, Processing of juices from exotic and minor fruits, enhancement of yields of mushrooms. Intellectual property rights bioproducts and biosafety with special reference to bioproducts and biosafety regulations.
13. Masters in Food processing—grain processing, bakery, coco products, soft drinks, alcoholic drinks, fruit and vegetable processing, milk and milk production, meat and poultry processing, fish processing, etc.
14. Masters in Human Resource Development with special reference to Food processing management and training (Degree, Diploma courses)
15. Degree/Diploma in non-conventional energy systems-biomass gasification, toilet linked plants, Community institutional and night soil based biogas plants program, Improved chulhas-models and implementation, Integrated rural energy program with special reference to basic rural needs for cooking, heating and lighting Solar Energy water

heating, solar cooking, air heating, building, shops. Solar photovoltaic program, Power from renewables—wind, biomass, solar, waste to energy. Urban and Industrial wastes and new technologies.

Technical Programs for Education and Outreach

Ecology on wide scale for moving an individual molecule to a global ecosystem for human resource development at all levels in human ecology.

- Two year postgraduate program in Human Ecology to prepare young men and women for managerial careers in developmental organization.
- One year (In-service, Pre-service) program for development practitioners aims to providing opportunities for young officers in rural development and producers' organizations to strengthen their professional management skills.
- Three months General Management Program provides opportunities to middle and senior level managers in rural producers ' cooperatives for mid-career reorientation and training.
- The six week Management Appraisal Program for Voluntary Agencies provided exposure to the management principles to people already involved in implementing and managing development programs.
- Short duration Management Development Programs, Seminars and Workshops bring a large number of developmental professionals to the department every year for specialized training for human resource management in the field of Human ecology.

Pre-service

In collaboration with Texas A&M University, Texas, USA

and College of Human Ecology, Michigan State University, USA.

1. M.Sc. Human Ecology, Biodiversity, Biotechnology and Environment Management

   Duration: 2 Yrs

   To equip all the students for graduate work for-

   (a) Career in industry, research laboratory and Government service

   (b) for students desiring entry into patent law and environmental studies

   (c) Professional health science programs and medical technology

   (d) Degree program for fulfilling necessary prerequisties of rural and underserved population through integrated population research and use of community focus health education and public service program.

2. M.Sc. in Women Agriculture and Rural Extension Management Duration: 1 Yr Curricula focus on teaching instructional programme and planning.

   (a) Under graduate certificate and degree programme to prepare the students for role as elementary and secondary teachers

   (b) Graduate system in the department contribute to the professional educators knowledge, based and prepare individuals for programme and instructional leadership roles and schools and other education setting including colleges and university.

   (c) Undergraduate degree in interdisciplinary technology

   (d) Masters and Doctoral degree include emphasis in adult and extension education, adult literacy distance, learning, industrial education, educational psychology HRD and technology education.

(e) Degree in agriculture education—M.Ed./ M.Sc.

(f) Allied health, teacher education and administration

(g) Master of science and counselling

3. Modification of B.Ed, and M.Ed, courses Duration: 1 year Collaboration with NCERT and Department of Education, Government. of India

For quality education by providing foundation links relevant in the market place and leadership development opportunities in collaboration with Lowry Mays College and Graduate School of Business.

Accounting, Business analysis and research, finance management, marketing and agribusiness.

Career-oriented Postgraduate degree programs in collaboration with University of Paisley, United Kingdom Distance Learning/On station programs-Real Estate Education, Master of Business Administration in Real Estate Management.

Core modules include: Integrated strategic resource 'Development of real estate, In-company real estate projects, Corporate real estate management' International Real-estate markets, and Real-estate investment analysis.

The course culminates in the MBA projects a practical in depth real-estate projects or relevance to a client organization.

Implementation of the program in collaboration between India and United Kingdom Universities as a result of the contact between India and British Scholars. (Under UGC Higher Education Link Programme)

In-service

Course on Women, Agriculture, Rural Extension, Biodiversity, Biotechnology

Collaboration with College of Human Ecology, Michigan State University, East Lansing, Michigan, USA.

Courses and training programs on agriculture education and life sciences leading to teacher certification

Duration: 3 Months, 1 year Tailor made programs

In service program will be developed in all collaboration with rural and underserved population through integrated and education research for training in on and off farm sectors for HRD with special reference to HRD.

CHAPTER 4

Women, Environment and Development

International Concern on Women Environment and Development, to Prepare Diverse Women for Diversity of Ecosystem

Human activities are changing the natural balance of the earth. Science aims at explaining things and events The process of science, which helps in searching the truth about nature, is guided by the facts, reasons and logics. Ecology is the study of the interactions between organisms and their environment. The scientific study of the relationship between plants and their environment merges into geography. Whereas Human Ecology is the interactions between human beings and their environment. It means to improve people's lives and environment with the focus on interactions of humans and its reciprocal effects that take place physically, socially, economically and aesthetically. The philosophy of human ecology provides the context for developing and serving the individuals and their families a productive quality of life To provide philosophical perspective to the "interdependence" in and among the various levels of social pyramid in the individuals at the top, the educational institutions, especially colleges have the unique distinction of being an institution of undergraduate, postgraduates and postgraduate studies to infuse "scientific temper" with an assortment of subjects from pure, applied and social sciences, befitting the students towards focused technical professional education to empower the community and women in particular through higher education, which aims to develop as well-rounded citizen, who is self confident, possess high professional and communicational skills and is committed to her role and responsibility in the society to safeguard on biodiversity.

Therefore, we must act fast to bring right institution in place for meeting eco-challenges in specific planning process and their direct enforcement in development process. It requires global co-operation to achieve the goal of sustainable development to deal with the critical theme of food, nutrition and environmental security. It also brings to center stage the need to help farm families to achieve utmost level of productivity, employment, income generation etc. Appropriate policies are evidently the most powerful instrument to accelerate economic development. Management of scientific research refers to "bottom up" approach to focus on need based approach and effective transfer. Voluntary private sector through the development and delivery of pad of packages for playing significant part both as catalyst and prime mover in rural development.

The main thrust will be directed towards youth employment, income generation and generation of mass awareness about development issues. The activities which are socially beneficial and economically viable like on-farm, off—farm and non farm will be taken up for the benefit of the community by doorstep and on-station technology transfer through short term training programme to ensure continuous benefits to the rural poor so that the resource and environment may be preserved for future generations.

Prioritization of Research Needs and Action Points for Functional Literacy to Deprives Through Training Programs and Door Step Technology Transfer

Empowerment of women for creation of an enabling environment where women can freely exercise their rights both within and outside home as equal partners

— generation of adequate human resource to meet the goal of promoting awareness, education through training and research programs in postgraduate courses, post doctoral program, short term training courses for service and in-service graduate, doorstep technology transfer.

— Development of education, linked to social education from primary school age through adulthood of all groups of people

— Enterprise resource planning-under university synergy programs.

To known better the human resource potential available in the region in order to develop not only national HRD plans but also to develop sub regional plans based on gaps analysis in supporting offered and to develop new mechanism for training.

Development of strategy for food production, income generation through genetic, bio-diversity, natural resource management and education to improve the environment of the community on sustainable basis.

- Provide support with action by providing a consistent internal policy, goals and links
- Provide leadership by taking part in linkage activities and giving them high visibility and priority
- Encourage the group for commitments towards the farming related activities
- Use mechanisms such as problem diagnoses, training and priority and set priorities
- Promotion the farming community farmer participation as collaborators and evaluators of alternatives technologies
- To college and circulate the information on training

programs to indeitfy common training needs in the country.

- To develop such as wen sites to further develop its training activities in research organizations and management in the regions.
- Sharing the management experience what ever the management structure, a measure of autonomy is essential in order to maintain flexibility, objectivity and responsiveness to stake holder a single nodal center handling research and education in agriculture together and able to coordinate effectively with other projects seen one model worthy of consideration. To ensure that research remains a profitable investment as well as to identify viable investment opportunities for research is important. However, public sector funded research institutions need to be aware of their purpose in research for public benefit so that benefit from collaborating with the private sector should not be captured entirely to private sectors.

Adaptation is also the mans linking imported technology with domestic R&D. Adaptation therefore, is that it is consonant with the strengthening of the capacity of effective acquisition and mastery of foreign technology as well as building up of an effective research and development system-an essential element of attempts to foster technological self reliance. Effective adaptation requires skilled manpower, which has atleast several years' experience in related production. The condition is not generally met in all but more advanced developing countries. The adaptation of technology however, is undertaken by engineers, technicians with an enterprise by industrial research institutions and by consulting engineers.

Absorption — the effective absorption and diffusion is dependent upon has an interest in applying the technology. The social carrier which has an interest in applying the technology. The social carrier could be a individual farmer who changes his pattern of production as a result of the introduction of improved plough. The carrier can be an institution. It might be an enterprise or agricultural cooperative that can develop can promote the new machinery and agro-technologies. Absorption of technology in a narrow sense could be facilitated by policies, accompanied by adequate training facilities both in terms of number of persons trained and in extent of training. Free horizontal mobility has also be ensured to the pool of trained personnels.

Towards Universal Education

In the third world countries rural areas are the places where majority of people live, pursuing age old traditional occupation like agriculture/cultivation. To food the hungry million, the only way left out is to increase or multiply productivity with majority of the population access to education is a matter of utmost significance not only for the upliftment of women but also for general betterment of society. The inclusion of eradication of illiteracy, the universities have accepted in principal the important place of extension world, besides teaching and research with the participation of 83 universities and over 200 colleges, most of the universities and colleges have been involved in varying degree of programs of eradication of illiteracy, population education and planing forums. Induction of other areas of extension such as rural development. Science for the people legal literacy, and environmental education has been undertaken. With the majority of population settled in rural countryside the development program should aim at generating income and employment to one and all. Access to education is a matter of utmost significance not only for the upliftment of women but also for the general betterment of society. Incidentally some of the programs with accent on women's participation have indirectly helped women to earn while indoors without distributing their normal house holds chores.

The development trends have picked up from macro level perspective. The filtration frames the wider Indian experiences in rural development wide range of theoretical inter-relations already settled in growth theory. With the formulation of UGC policy frame 1977 a process of involving university system as such to participate extension programs was initiated with the specific objective of securing equal importance of extension as a third dimension with teaching and research. Though some universities were conducting continuing education programs and universities involved in substantial way in the National Adult education program of Govt. of India. However, the infra structure is too inadequate even for minimum performance for institutionalizing need based extension programs to involve identified communities in the life long learning process yet not operationalized in most cases.

Institutionalization of extension needs academic acceptance which is automatically ensured when the activities enter at a stage of studies and research which enlarges our under standing and contributes to the knowledge. Extension activities can enter into research through project work or field based dissertations at under graduate and postgraduate level will be forced to burn dried animal dung and agricultural crop residue, there by further decreasing food crop yields. The potentially valuable fire wood crops that deserve increased recognition on species suitable for growing firewood for individual firewood for individual family needs. However species suited to plantation cultivation for fueling and industrial factories, electric generators and crop dries are also considered. Most of the plants are little known in traditional forest production. Some are woody shrubs rather than forest trees, but even those many branched, crocked some time short lived species many meet many requirements for small scale village use, to such characteristics as: Nitrogen fixing ability, rapid growth, ability of coppice, ability to produce, wood of high calorific value that burns without spark or toxic smoke and ability to go successful to a wide range of environments, including different attitudes soil types, rain fall regions, amount of sun light.

Keeping in mind those sites now causing the greatest concern: where fuel wood has virtually disappeared. It concentrates on new plantings. These re, however, large areas where tree resources still exists that, with careful husbandary, could be maintained as fuel resources. Moreover, there is scope for harvesting fire wood as a by product for industrial logging and of conventional plantation forestry. The potential for producing fuel from these conditions is also important to consider.

An alternative and complementary approach to the fire wood crises is the substitution of well designed stoves or boilers for the generally in efficient devices now widely used.

Unconventional scientific research with promise for fire wood include studies of fast growing tropical grasses as fuel crops and some exceptionally promising fire wood species are related technologies are Leucaena, promising forage and tree crops of tropics, tropical legumes, resources for future. Producer gas—a little known fuel for motor transport, sowing forest-by broad casting seeds in any trials of fuel wood plantations local species should always be given first priority.

A case study of village Chauawali (Uttar Pradesh) based on Studies in relation to fuel yield, sponsored by Department of Non Conventional Energy Sources. The need based crops like Cajuns cajan which has multiple uses and fits well in the corporate style of the far house-holds is an example to link between need and socio cultural setting is a complex system still the farming system aimed at harmonizing social and economic objectives with ecologically sound management Based on the principles of self reliance, satisfaction of basic needs has proved quite appropriate new symbiosis of man on earth. To make it more adaptive constant education and training is needed to realize that a mismatch between a food crop and land cost us 6 to 12 months but a similar mistake in forestry will cost us one generation. If it has to succeed there will have to be participation of people; building up of an information base and above all treating forestry as S&T activity.

Conservation of biological diversity: the biological wealth of the country is very rich with nearly 45,000 plants, and 65,000 animal species. However, our efforts are conservation has been directed to the conservation more correctly preservation of big cats, as also some large animals, crocodile, birds etc. and we have ignored all together plants, forests trees in particular, as also micro organisms and mangroves and marine biological wealth. There is major lacuna in our efforts. Even in the case of big cats, the stress has been on the art of wild life rather that he science of wild life. All conservation efforts have to be directed to keep the species away from decline. To ensure conservation in space and time, we need to have strategy based on principles of genetic and evolutionary biology. We are far from it. To base the conservation efforts on an ecosystem basis and not only species basis we must take expeditious action and establish, the Biosphere reserves. These are areas of vital importance to the country. A gene rich country such as ours, will be left behind if when we have the expertise and experience second to none in the world in this area.

Infect university system has never been encouraged enter the research and development to take science based conservation of natural sites as also the biological diversity in plants, especially forest trees, animals and micro organisms on land in water, and marine environments.

METHODOLOGY

To be concerned with man in the social world it is necessary to explore the reality which underlines and characterizes 'man', the 'social', and 'world'. Philosophy is inescapable for the social scientist who seeks clarity and rigour in work, who takes the term 'methodology' seriously. It is not merely a question of interest in the logic of scientific enquiry, a matter of paying attention to the status of propositions, models and laws. For paying attention to the phenomena of the social world, symbolism and meaning of social action; men acting in the context of an inter-subjective reality, shared and sustained by temporal beings aware of themselves no less than each other.

A crucial aspect of methodology relates to the relationship between the observer and the observed. A host of philosophical problems concerning the nature of the subject, subjectivity, construction of the subject, and in consequence textual construction of subject, but also of consciously trying to enter into the world of meanings of the subjects under study. The phenomenological critique of sociology has stressed the fact that data gathering is a social process and needs to be understood as such.

With regards to various approaches to methodology that are open today. For anyone looking back over the preceding survey," the most striking fact remains the dominance of the positivist tradition in methodological writing and its influence in the form of the desire for adoption of the 'methods of science'. This has meant, in practice, the devising of a particular mode of enquiry stressing the importance of concepts, hypotheses linked to defined variables, empirical testing and formal analysis. In conjunction with this process social statistics have been used to aid both in the construction of the empirical test and in the analysis and interpretation of the results. The other themes that emerge from the alternative tradition which has been based in social anthropology, village and community studies.

While exploring the themes attempt has been made to

identify their problems and implications. These are issues related not simply to techniques of research, but also to the questions of meaning in an inter-subjective world, justification of applying statistical logic and experimental method to a post-positivist universe, nations of objectivity, science reality and realism, methodological implications of construction of subject and test and so on. The general tenor of methodological texts has been to provide a stereotyped account of 'scientific' method, research design, hypotheses, observation, interview in an uncritical fashion, following the model of scientism and without in any way in-corporating the current views of these subjects.

The problem that arises in this kind of work concerns the nature of conceptual categories to be employed and this kind of research method has the inherent danger of allowing the social scientist of negate his vital function of making sense if the data, of consciously constructing the problem rather than expecting it to emerge at some later stage.

Our aim is to go beyond mere descriptions of various methods, to examine the theory, logic and philosophy of the methods and to explore their implications. The questions of methodology proper are linked both with the theoretical issues related to philosophy and to applied issues associated with various mathematical and quantitative techniques. At an abstract level, questions of method and questions of theory overlap and are often identical. They are related to various theoretical positions like positivism, phenomenology. Structuralism, post-structuralism and so on. The first task, therefore, is to look at some of the main elements in methodology and how they have been put into operation in the research process.

In the typical methodology text, the 'traditional method' is contrasted with the 'scientific method', and described as something prohibiting proper research. For instance, this is how the features of the traditional methods have been described (i) methodological adhocims (ii) eminence of subjective perception (iii) ethical preoccupation rooted in the refusal to distinguish methodologically between facts and values, between 'is' and 'ought', (iv) the dominance of quality against quantity, and (v) the grater use of intuition and imagination, which are regarded as essentially disruptive of modern scientific methodology, are the constituents of the traditional method. The conventional methodology is based on the notion of 'scientific objectivity', which is related to bias in social science.The problem of scientific objectivity is still worsened because of the bias of the social scientists governed by conscious or unconscious political and social attitudes and values.

Field Work Methodology

Fieldwork approach in principle rejects the positivist assumption that descriptive concepts are simply a first stage towards the test of explanatory hypotheses. The concern for interpretation of culture and meaning and interest in practices through which social relations become visible form the basis of fieldwork methods. In contrast with the sharp distinction between concepts and explanatory hypotheses within the positivist approach, in the interactions and interpretative fieldwork method 'understanding' the actions and interactions of respondents by virtue of grasping and comprehending the culturally appropriate concept through which the people conduct their social life, is the way in which the explanation is achieved. In the fieldwork method the focus is on naturally occurring situation, the encounters that people have in normal course of events. In this way, it is hoped to produce descriptions and explanations appropriate to the ways in which people actually behave.

There is no dearth of books on research methodology, and almost all aim teaching the novice statistical methods, survey research and its history, drawing up different kinds of questionnaires, interviewing, opinion polls, content analysis and market surveys. Scientific method in the social sciences, in which the need is stressed for the clear formulation of hypotheses to be tested in the inquiry, appropriate research design, the elimination of bias in the collection and interpretation data etc. Throughout, the assumption appears that the social sciences are of the same character as the natural sciences'. The new developments in social anthropology, in their view, have blurred the distinction between anthropology and sociology, particularly so in India. Though in methodological terms a conceptual distinction can be made between ethnographic field work and participant observation in which the former involves a recognition of the interdependence of theoretical and methodological issues and the latter relates more to description in terms of participation which often trivialize the issue involved to one meter technique. Like the discussions of how to obtain access and or to remain concealed and so on-in Indian fieldwork literature no such distinction is made.

The account of fieldwork cover a very wide range of field situations and subjects. The varied locale and subjects cover slums, factories, trade union, industrial cooperatives, college students, school, hospital, minorities, nomads, small towns, and of course, villages. The accounts also point out some important aspects of fieldwork, which are not generally discussed in the available textbooks. However, the field work account argue that hypotheses cannot be formulated in a vacuum, without knowledge of the field. Moreover, the fieldworkers cannot anticipate the developments in the field, which will inevitably guide the course of his investigation. Hypotheses formed without regard to these considerations may turn out to be trivial if bot banal. Almost no contribution to this volume has been guided by hypotheses, and some confess that their theorizing was only post facts. What most fieldwork do is to go to the field with a founding in the theory of the discipline, especially in the sub-area of their interest, and with as much knowledge of the region as can be derived from secondary material. The field situation offers him opportunities to reformulate existing concepts and invest them with new meaning.

Survey Methodology

One of the commonly used methods in empirical social science research in India is the survey method. The theme concern how survey research must be designed and conducted as an institution of first accounting of the great variability within them, and second becoming more relevant to the social cultural environment within which measurement occurs. Subordinated to these key issues, the need for using complementary research methods to support and enrich surveys; the need for pre-study exploration prior to conducting the full study; the significance of human errors; the act non-randomly to bias and thereby weaken the survey methodology; the need to study non-random sources and types of biases and describe these methodological findings so that study can be replicated and socio-economic feasibility of implementing results be know.

Inductive Methodology

Provide the basis for research methods can be described as deductive nomological and inductive-statistical system attempts to provide a basis for unification of the sciences and also embodies certain specific features of positivism.

Systems of Social Indicators

With the increasing demand for the present day literature dealing with social policy for the development of systems of social indicators various methodologies have been geared for developing appropriate measures.

Mathematics: Computers and Formal Analysis

A body of theory in sociology and anthropology that

does not call for mathematical treatment, for any theory that conceives of society or culture as a system is committed to the notion of interrelationship of parts, and all conceptions of the cultural consensus and conformity on the one hand and degree of complexity on the other can involve nations of formal analysis, of measure and sealer arrangement as their abstract representations.

Human Ecology for Globalization of Agriculture for Community Based Approaches

Man's relationship with his environment now occupies a major place among the problems agitating mankind. Therefore it is necessary to demonstrate the scientific programmes in a way towards meeting the sustainable and safe future to mankind.

Our life depends on one thing called oneself. Who is the self is an important truth to be arrived at. To know and not to act on what you know is equal to not knowing. If you have not acted then you have not known. Not knowing is ignorance. People fall in love with words and concepts. We have started loving words and not action. We have started believing that a word is knowledge and not action. Treat action as knowledge and not words. We live in jargons; we give power in words. We should learn to give power in action to treat action as wisdom and not words as wisdom. The wisdom will grow with the power. It teaches us that less be use our power the greater it will be. There will be no end to the troubles of states, or of humanity itself till philosophers become kings in the world. The political power and philosophy thus come into the same hands. It is an illusion that we are one—the person we assume ourselves to be and what we really are. If we observe ourselves can we see that we are the observer and part of us is observed or else the observer pollutes the observations and creates an imaginary self.

It is an imposing status—the aquiline features of great

educationist visionary gazing far into the distance—and fitting for one of the greatest universities in the world. To solve in and to make sure that it is for real global terror and communal tension on seven sins of public life—Politics without principles, wealth without work, pleasure without consciousness, knowledge without character, commerce without morality, science without humanity and worship without sacrifice. We have to notice that the way we walk, talk, think, feel, criticise, praise, like, dislike. If we notice these movements closely our life will start transforming itself mysteriously. Also it will guide us to demonstrate effectively the sustainable solutions of healthy communities.

Human Ecology is the study of interaction between human beings and their environment. It is a means to improve people's lives and human environment emphasizing the study of reciprocal effects that take place physically, socially, economically and aesthetically. The philosophy of human ecology provides the context for developing and serving the individuals and their families from a human environment perspective towards building the sustaining productive quality of life.

The concept of ecology by way of introducing the field of botany to contribute to international research in relation to other sciences for rural development, human resource development and promotion of education and economic interest for all sections of society. It combines the interest, theories and studies of geographer, ecologist, agricultural scientist, economist and biologist for the major themes:

- Linking higher education for community service.
- Changes required in the area of Home Science programmes to make them relevant to all sections of society.
- Setting priorities in research to help community in the area of agribusiness, biodiversity and

environment, biotechnology, non-conventional energy systems and human resource development.

Indian Council for Agricultural Research (ICAR) proposed new division of Human Ecology at Delhi University for the establishment of new faculty for Human Ecology for research, education, extension and outreach with the fund support of ICAR, Department of Agriculture Cooperation (DAC) and Food and Agricultural Organization of United Nation (FAO), New Delhi (In partnership for international linkages):

- Home Science to Human Ecology for graduate programmes to investigate the interaction of people across life span with their natural, social and designed environments in partnership with College of Human Ecology, Michigan State University and Texas A&M (U.S.).
- Establishment of Department of Human Ecology for international linkages in partnership with school of environment resources and development, Bangkok, Thailand. For interdisciplinary approach for making difference in society with School of Social Sciences, Middlesex University (U.K.) for postgraduate and post experience programmes on criminology, social policy, psychology, geography and environmental management, social science research methods, social work and research degree for social science support including taught master programmes, M. Phil and Ph.D. Underpinned by teaching and research training for lively research culture focused around conferences, seminars, forums and other activities together with the lectures from invited speakers. In partnership with Wageningen University, The Netherlands to interact with environment in environment management, Bio-technology, Food Science & Technology, Forest and natural conservation, geo-information science,

consumer studies and modeling tools for environment and resource management, water supply, drainage and sewerage engineering.

Mission. Strengthening and empowering individuals and families to interact effectively with their environment.

Vision. To meet the society needs, to develop unique culture by linking several disciplines and professionals for ecology of individuals, families in their diverse socio cultural, physical, biological environment where diversity of ecosystem is a way of life.

CHAPTER 5

Education in Human Ecology

Growing activities of human and his increasing demands on the biotic and a biotic components of environment has brought forth a change in his ecological philosophy. He is now directing his attention more on the study of habitat or ecological system as a whole than on their components. The biotic components are just a small past of habitat or ecological systems. In order to study the environment and micro changes brought in various components *i.e.,* water, air and soil, we study the climate and edifice elements. The distribution, adaptations and functional aspects of the organisms and communities are studied in greater details in ecology and relevant information is obtained from biological literature on biogeography systematic cytology, genetics and physiology.

It is, therefore, imperative for an ecologist to be acquainted with various disciplines of physical and biological sciences in order to get integrated picture of the environmental complex in relation to organic world.

Human ecology is the study of interaction between human beings and their environment. It is a means to improve people's life and environment, a emphasising in depth study of reciprocal effects that takes place physically, socially economically and esthetically. Its basic approach is the conservation of natural resources both renewable and non-renewable and interlinks the science of biology as an interpretative science and elucidates the existence in the environment. It comes with the system that supports man.

Life on our planet originated much earlier than man came into existence. Mental set up of man has made him a super animal. *Man* is no longer slaving to the environment but through his technical skills he has to attain, he has to certain extended attained mastery over his environment. He creates favourable environment for his welfare in doing so, many a times, he forgets that his is a small component of nature and by disturbing nature and by disturbing the environmental balance, he is inviting trouble, change of forests, building roads and dames, industrial set ups and urbanisation, server and waste disposal etc., are some of the activities which are rapidly changing environments of our planet.

The paradigms of biodiversity conservation, which is, held by community whose survival and sustenance is linked to local biodiversity utilisation and conservation. For local indigenous communities, conserving biodiversity means to conserving biodiversity means to conserve the integrity of ecosystem and species, the right of those resources and knowledge, and their production systems based on biodiversity. For them biodiversity has intrinsic value as well as high use value.

The utilisation of biodiversity in people's economy is guided by a plurality of knowledge systems. The implementation of these properties, characteristics and use of this biodiversity is held with the local communities in different languages, and in their diverse epistemological frameworks.

Nature's diversity and diversity of knowledge system is however, undergoing a major or process of destabilisation with the expansion of patents and intellectual property rights into the domain of biodiversity via the TRIPs Agreement of the World Trade Organisation. It is totally inadequate for the objectives of protection and conservation of biodiversity on one hand and protection of our indigenous intellectual heritage and social creativity on the other hand. Changes in our policy and law are being made with respect to our biological and intellectual heritage. The plant variety legislation is being introduced by the environment ministry.

No Ministry is addressing the unique problems associated with the objective of conservation of medicinal plant biodiversity and protection of indigenous systems of medicines and their practitioners especially in the context of TRIPs. The framework law for implementation of Biodiversity conservation can therefore, be covered in a legal framework, appropriate to the domain of biodiversity and indigenous knowledge for protecting our biological and intellectual heritage. In the absence of Biodiversity legislation to perpetuate the piracy as intellectual property rights of western laboratories and corporation, will function as one-sided legislation. Protecting our biological and intellectual heritage in the age of biopiracy requires the recognition and rejuvenation of our heritage and the evolution of legal system for the protection of this heritage in the context of emerging IPR regimes needed globally to prevent piracy.

To promote changes in the way the centre and states develop and employ human resources with the aim to make them and their sectors more productive and to modernise its agricultural sector at Nodal Centre for Human Ecology. To achieve these changes, policy and institutional reform would be carried out. The project would foster changes in the investment priorities resulting from policy and institutional reforms will focus on the process of : (a) improving the quality and relevance of higher education for community service through training programmes, and (b) strengthening the capacity of participating states to develop and manage agricultural human resource.

To upgrade human resource management the project at

state level would support development and management programmes (HRD & HRM) including training focused on job oriented needs for (i) Systematic need assessment, (ii) training and trainers, (iii) evaluation of training-effectiveness, (iv) better instructional facilities, and (v) improve management of state sector employees. This will redress environmental degradation, desirable resources and environment management practices, common property resource management, improve management skills, self-sustaining capacity, employment generation, mass awareness, income generation. The activities which are socially beneficial and economically viable like on-farm, off-farm and non-farm will be undertaken for the benefit of the community by doorstep and on-station technology transfer for functional literacy, through short term training programmes to ensure continues benefit to rural poor so that the resource and environment may be preserved for future generation.

EDUCATION AND TRENDS IN CURRICULA

Vocational/Career Oriented Programmes

Empowering people at different socio-economic and educational levels, which are appropriate to market demand both in rural and urban areas. For students who have undergone general education courses in continuing education could offer specific skills, for those already in job to update skills or acquire qualifications for career advancement.

The school curricula of 1960s had elements of ecology and conservation of nature and its resources right from primary stage to biology courses of middle, secondary or senior secondary classes. The approach of integrating the teaching of science, social science even the mathematics and language with experience of children was extended to upper primary and secondary stage as part of general education. The environmental concept problems and introduction of social and environmental studies provided teachers with a curricular area in which the need and interest of children could be met through a focus on the local environment. Students must be given the opportunity to develop the sense of ownership, and empowerment so that they are fully invested in an environmental sense and motivated to become responsible active citizens.

Yeshpal Committee Report 1993 strongly recommended Gandhian approach to learning. Many other institutions in different parts of the country use different approaches and methodologies with same results. What runs through them all is the thread of spirituality and ecological thinking. All these institutions is still value education through course work as well as practices. It would be in fact appropriate to describe the institutional framework for training and research in sociology, which as emerged after independence. Sociology in India is largely a discipline of borrowed concepts and methods derived from high prestige centres of learning in affluent wet especially in the USA and UK. this has resulted in chasing high prestige models into quick sand of pseudo-intellection. Sociologists have still not related themselves directly to the people and their problems and still revelling in counter productive intellectualism. Our sociology does not address itself to the living concern of today and tomorrow. As a result it is not able to contribute meaningfully towards resolving many dilemmas of development.

The concept of human resource system therefore assumes that human being is great asset in the organisation. They are not merely necessarily evils to be reckoned with but they can contribute a great deal to the achievement of organisational as an asset with the unlimited potential in the concept of Human Resource Systems. The study of people at most is generally referred to as the study of organisational behaviour. It is the systematic study of the actions and attitude that people exhibit within organisation. The field of organisational behaviour (OB) is based on large number of systematically designed research studies. An organisation is a formal structure of planned coordination involving two or more people in order to achieve in common goal.

Contributing Disciplines

Organisational behaviour is applied behaviour science and as a result, is built upon contributions from several behaviours discipline. The predominant are psychology, sociology, social psychology, anthropology and political science. Psychology's contribution has been mainly at individual or micro level of analysis, whereas the latter disciplines have contributed to our understanding of macro concepts — group processes and organisational behaviour. The psychology explains or sometimes changes the behaviour of humans and other animals. The goals of human behaviour studies are concerned with developing people's skills, help to explain, predict and control human behaviour. The human behaviour studies after technologies that facilitate the control of people. In fact whether these technologies should be used in organisation becomes ethical question. The control objectives are frequently seen by managers as the most valuable contribution that human behaviour makes towards effectiveness on the jobs. Today's managers understand that the success of any effort at improving quality and productivity must include their employees. These employees will only be major force in changing out the changes and will actively participate in planning other changes.

Improving People's Skill

The relevant theory and concepts that can help one, plan and predicts the behaviour of people. These are variety of ways to motivate people, how to be better communicator and how to create more effective team to be used in the job.

Motivating the Workforce

Reconstituted into job requiring considerable higher

technical skills or taking workers in other countries that will do the same work for a fraction of the wages. In this situation employee tends to perform either low skilled jobs or higher skilled jobs that means to maintain a middle class or upper class life style. This situation leads to a major challenge for managers. How to motivate who are making very low wage and have very little opportunity to significantly increase their pay either in current or through promotion.

System Development and Research

Various systems for human resource systems need to be continuously designed, tested and reviewed. Data being collected also need to be analysed to give dues to the developing interventions. Development of human resource system can be conceived a system with interlinkages amongst its various components. The central concern of various components of HRS seems to be job. Job is defined in terms of critical attributes, background characteristics necessary like education and training and experience person has before he takes up the job we get training needs out of the critical attributes which also contribute to the concept of career planning of education and training. If we further expand we get into several new directions. The concept of human resource management is an approach to the management of the people. The behavioural science movement made two useful contributions to HRM.

Organisation development movement. The organisational development (OD) movement advocated the implementation of programmes designed to improve the effectiveness with which organisation functions and responds to change, with particular emphasis on how people carry out their work and interest with one another. The total approach to organisational behaviour exerted a strong influence on many of these who in the late 70's and early 80's began concentrate on corporate culture as a central issue in the management of human resource.

Different organisations have different traditions. In some

organisations personal function may already include some aspects like general administration such as general administration such special features will certainly influence the design of some aspect of HRS. The traditional factor where HRS was designed was part of the personal function. Where HRS was introduced, administration was also put along with the department was designated human resource administration.

Challenges and Opportunities

The human behaviour studies solutions or at least some meaningful insights towards solutions. The relevant concepts and theories that can help one, plan and predict. Each organisation has its own tradition. These influence the design of human, resource systems. If an organisation is highly centralised the designs will be own kind; if its is decentralised, the design would be quite different.

Transfer of Technology

The process of transfer of technology cannot be examined in isolation. The effectiveness of TOT is greatly influenced by the linkages between and among those responsible for technology generation. The process of TOT could be examined wholly taking the process as major systems and the research extension client and input sub systems and its component. Prioritisation of research needs and action points for functional literacy to deprive through training programmes and doorstep technology transfer.

Empowerment of women for creation of an enabling environment where women can freely exercise their rights both within and outside home as equal partners :

— generation of adequate human resource to meet the goal of promoting awareness, education through training and research programmes in postgraduate courses, post doctoral programme, short term training courses for service and in-service graduate, doorstep technology transfer.

— Development of education, linked to social education from primary school age through adulthood of all groups of people.

— Enterprise resource planning — under university synergy programmes.

To known better the human resource potential available in the region in order to develop not only national HRD plans but also to develop sub regional plans based on gaps analysis in supporting offered and to develop new mechanism for training.

Development of strategy for food production, income generation through genetic, bio-diversity, natural resource management and education to improve the environment of the community on sustainable basis.

- Provide support with action by providing a consistent internal policy, goals and links.
- Provide leadership by taking part in linkage activities and giving them high visibility and priority.
- Encourage the group for commitments towards the farming related activities.
- Use mechanisms such as problem diagnoses, training and priority and set priorities.
- Promotion the farming community, farmer participation as collaborators and evaluators of alternatives technologies.
- To collect and circulate the information on training programmes to identify common training needs in the country.
- To develop such as web sites to further develop its training activities in research organisations and management in the regions.

- Sharing the management experience whatever the management structure, a measure of autonomy is essential in order to maintain flexibility, objectivity and responsiveness to stakeholder; a single nodal centre handling research and education in agriculture together and able to coordinate effectively with other projects seen one model worthy of consideration. To ensure that research remains a profitable investment as well as to identify viable investment opportunities for research is important. However, public sector funded research institutions need to be aware of their purpose in research for public benefit so that benefit from collaborating with the private sector should not be captured entirely to private sectors.

Adaptation — is also the man's linking imported technology with domestic R&D. Adaptation therefore, is that it is consonant with the strengthening of the capacity of effective acquisition and mastery of foreign technology as well as building up of an effective research and development system — an essential element of attempts to foster technological self-reliance. Effective adaptation requires skilled manpower, which has atleast several years' experience in related production. The condition is not generally met in all but more advanced developing countries. The adaptation of technology however, is undertaken by engineers, technicians with an enterprise by industrial research institutions and by consulting engineers.

Absorption — the effective absorption and diffusion is dependent upon has an interest in applying the technology. The social carrier which has an interest in applying the technology. The social carrier could be a individual farmer who changes his pattern of production as a result of the introduction of improved plough. The carrier can be an institution. It might be an enterprise or agricultural cooperative that and develop can promote the new machinery and agro technologies. Absorption of technology in a narrow sense could be facilitated by policies, accompanied by adequate training facilities both in terms of number of persons trained and in extent of training. Free horizontal mobility has also been ensured to the pool of trained personnels.

Towards Universal Education

In the third world countries rural areas are the places where majority of people live, pursuing age old traditional occupation like agriculture/cultivation. To food the hungry million, the only way left out is to increase or multiply productivity with majority of the population access to education is a matter of utmost significance not only for the upliftment of women but also for general betterment of society. The inclusion of eradication of illiteracy, the universities have accepted in principal the important place of extension world, besides teaching and research with the participation of 83 universities and over 200 colleges, most of the universities and colleges have been involved in varying degree of programmes of eradication of illiteracy, population education and planning forums. Induction of other areas of extension such as rural development. Science for the people legal literacy, and environmental education has been undertaken. With the majority of population settled in rural countryside the development programme should aim at generating income and employment to one and all. Access to education is a matter of utmost significance not only for the upliftment of women but also for the general betterment of society. Incidentally some of the programmes with accent on women's participation have indirectly helped women to earn while indoors without distributing their normal households chores.

The development trends have picked up from macro level perspective. The filtration frames the wider Indian experiences in rural development wide range of theoretical inter-relations already settled in growth theory. With the formulation of UGC policy frame 1977 a process of involving university system as such to participate extension programmes was initiated with the specific objective of securing equal importance of extension as a third dimension with teaching and research. Though some universities were conducting continuing education programmes and universities involved in substantial way in the National Adult education programme of Government of India. However, the infra structure is too inadequate even for minimum performance for institutionalising need based extension programmes to involve identified communities in the life long learning process yet not operationalised in most cases.

Institutionalisation of extension needs academic acceptance which is automatically ensured when the activities enter at a stage of studies and research which enlarges our understanding and contributes to the knowledge. Extension activities can enter into research through project work or field based dissertations at undergraduate and postgraduate level.

Asian Centre for Human Ecology Foundation

To conduct, coordinate and promote relevant agricultural research and education in order to contribute to over all agricultural development on a sustainable basis, through effective research leadership, capacity building and UGC policy formulations :

- To recognise the outstanding contributions of institutions.
- To recognise at various stages of scientists professional carrier.
- For postgraduate agricultural research at Ph.D. level.

In order to promote research for tribal areas and applied research, to encourage post doctoral research to promote multidisciplinary and inter institutional team research at national level for excellence in teaching at Internation Centre of Human Ecology, South Campus :

- To promote the technology assessment, refinement and transfer process and playing the pro-active role in evolving and implementing the new policy initiative. For institutions and scientists to avail themselves of such vast opportunities to contribute significantly in their chosen profession to maintain the sanctity to peep into the professional qualities of all time and placing the thrust to watch how they reached the pinnacles of their chosen carrier in life with awe and inspiration.
- To encourage the young scientist to learn and imbibe those great qualities, processing them in a time bound manner requires the cooperation of so many sections/ individuals at the Asian Centre for Human Ecology from administration, accounts, audit, transport, publicity deserve special mention.
- To establish strong higher educational programmemes in specialised areas of national global relevance such as biotechnology and molecular biology environmental sciences, agribusiness management, post harvest technology, information technology, communication development, remote sensing, non conventional energy sources, disease forecasting etiology etc.
- The trained human resource development and to have a comprehensive picture of agricultural systems of India in collaboration with the institutions of higher learning of agricultural sciences (33 state agricultural universities, 5 deemed to be universities including Allahabad Agricultural Institutes, one Central Agricultural University, Imphal, 3 Central Universities (BHU, AMU &

Vishwa Bharti) and 50 developed requisite expertise to meet the future challenges, owing to the nonavailability of composite data base on institutions, programmemes, eligibility conditions etc., national scenario on agricultural education has rather been somewhat pre summative.

- The publication developed would be a useful document for the students, professionals and policy makers and would enable the readers to have a comprehensive picture.

To Conduct the Programme and Institutions of Their Choice

- To help such students in making options for a programme and university.
- To compile information on carrier opportunities available in agricultural sciences.
- To update information by the universities in supplying pertinent information to their universities depicting eligibility conditions intake capacity and other academic regulations at SAUs, DUS.
- To be our endeavour a new initiative to improve the quality of education in order to reduce in breeding, inculcate spirit of healthy competition and improve cultural life at the campuses, which include admission to seats at UG level, at PG entrance examinations and award of National Talent Scholarships, Junior Research fellowships on the basis of merit.
- To focus on 11 disciplines at undergraduate level such as B.Sc. Agriculture, B.Sc Horticulture, B.Sc (Fishery)/ BFSc., B.Sc Forestry, B.Sc Home Science, B.Sc Sericulture, B.Tec (DT)/ B.Sc (DT), B.Tec (AE), B.Sc (Food Science and Technology), B.Sc (B&C) and BVSc & AH.

Objectives

- To meet a strong base of agricultural education.
- To meet and to make it suitable fulfilment of immediate as well as further requirements of agriculture in the country.
- To be recognised as national issue in phase manner Delhi State autonomous status to the institution offering agricultural education.
- Location of home science and relevant technological education at the same campus.
- Integration of teaching by offering courses in any of the institution to provide holistic teaching on semester, trimester based internal evaluation.
- Integration of education, research and extension education.

As a centre of higher education and training in agricultural sciences at national and international level :

- To conduct basic and strategic researches with a view of understanding the processes, in all their complexity and to undertake need based research and sustained agricultural productivity in harmony with the environment.
- To serve as a centre for academic excellence in the area of postgraduate education and human resource development in agricultural sciences.
- To provide national leadership in agricultural research, extension and technology assessment and transfer by developing new concepts and approaches and serving as a national referral point for quality and standards.
- To develop information systems, add value to information share and serve the information nationally and serve as a data base.

Duration of the Degree Programme

The duration of all educational programmes in 4 yrs. with 6 months compulsory internship.

Eligibility Qualifications

- Broadly students with science (Physics, Chemistry) at 10+2 with biology and/or mathematics are eligible for admission for programmes in Human Ecology in University of Delhi. The courses imparted outside SAUs system in order to vocationalisation of agricultural education to prepare a vast network of para-professionals in diversified areas of agricultural practices especially in faculties of Agriculture, Home Sciences, Horticulture, Veterinary Sciences, Fishery and Forestry. To incorporate new courses on information technology environmental sciences, library sciences, biostatics, biotechnology, biodiversity in all degree programmes to further strengthen skill base training in women agriculture training for one semester have been made integral component of degree programmes. The students undergoing WARE get slipped during the training period.

Asian Centre for Human Ecology

Action mechanism for imparting education and training to the students to develop into centre of academic excellence with latest facilities available in the country, for the formulation of action plan for major activities to bear nexus to the objective and project benefit for :

- Expenditure schedule for each activities and if possible duration and sequence of events for the advancement of student community action and rural/urban slum technology in implementing welfare and development programmes, welfare activities including sensitising organising and mobilising people at village community level.

- To set a common forum for exchange of information, work out modalities for sharing of resources, experience and expertise and evolve strategies and guiding principle for community empowerment through participatory processes leading to social change.
- In order to facilitate the process of networking, NGOs working for children and women for two-way flow of information from voluntary sector to a nodal point in government sector to develop modalities to strengthen the ongoing programmes for children and women, and identify innovative and replicable community based approaches.
- Strengthening interdepartmental and government NGO linkages for integrated women and child.
- Networking for promotion of child health and nutrition.
- Strengthen research on women's role in agriculture, food security and focus issues specifically on alliance with women in development programmes.
- Bringing researchers together in the field.
- Breaking down disciplinary barriers.
- Approach, basic to on-farm research.
- Interdisciplinary team work in the subsequent stages of research process to identify constraints.

For the Projects for the Development of Infrastructure for Women, Agriculture and Rural Extension

- For the relevance of education, equity and access of management of higher education.
- UGC administration for "financial mechanism"
- For the cause of : The training for the future :

- — The asset way-industry acceptance of asset of the student community.
- — Promotion of ecologically sustainable agriculture.
- — Carry out agricultural research relevant to social sciences including statics, economics, extension, Home Science and Nutrition. Sustainable and equitable use of agro-biodiversity.
- — Eco development concerns in Natural agricultural farming system, R&D approaches.

To meet the emerging demands for — productivity, sustainability, and environmental and ecological security. To coordinate research with the community perception education and reforms.

For the Cause of Linkages

National. To implement most of its programmes through the ICAR Institutes, Research organisations, NGOs with whom it has strong linkages. These linkages will be further nurtured and strengthened by its fellows in the projects and Institutions.

International. To promote collaborative activities in the areas of agricultural research for modalities of cooperation. To establish bilateral linkages.

Indian experience in rural development and examines it in the frame of wide range of theoretical inter-relations already settled in Growth Theory. It draws considerably from historical evidences to reach the policy-making part of analysis.

DIVERSITY FOR LOCAL ACTION AND ULTIMATE ANSWER

Despite the occasional Hindu flavour, the core philosophy of Bastar's tribals remains charmingly untouched.

- Life is friendship; to live to have friendship why should

we quarrel? We should show mercy to everyone, starting with trees, the tribal might have added. For wasn't trees it sheltered Ram during his *Van Vas?* And which metaphorically, still shelter us today from the spiritual wastelands that threatens to engulf us?

Science attempts to define the nature of reality. Reality however, presents itself in variety of names and forms : Physical mental and psychological realities; linguistic and mathematical reality. But science is yet to define physical reality conclusive... hence the quest continues....

If there are so many realities, what then is absolute reality? Spiritual Science or adhyatma is concerned with the understanding of this absolute reality which the Vedas call Brahman and which we refer as to God or paramatma.

The central focus in all the six Indian language system namely Sankya, Yoga, Nyaya Visheshika, Purva Mimansa or Vedanta is to answer this question and present the experimental knowledge of absolute reality by perceiving pure joy everywhere through speech and action by expanding our 'I'ness spanning the entire universe. By seeing one self in all names and forms of objective reality and by believing in and discovering one's own and every one else's infinite nature and infinite capabilities; being pure in body, mind and intellect. So to find God and have to find our own self. Ultimately reality presents itself as our pure and infinite self.

ESTABLISHMENT OF ASIAN CENTRE FOR HUMAN ECOLOGY

India was first among global community to have a national policy population. Today we strive for perfection in every field with the evolution of mind and intellect worldly knowledge has become easily accessable. So, we have achieved certain measures of excellence in the physical sciences but physical experience fails to connect with our true self to shoulder our education in India have collaborated with many Indian foreign Universities for helping them and designing the curriculum on environment at graduate and postgraduate levels. The idea behind is to search the grass root level with the view to implement programmes at global level for making them worldly. Catch young for generation of eco-fragile biodiversity and making them aware of the need to protect our mother earth.

Sustainability is fundamentally an ethic that of reverence for all life forms and respect for their rights to exist to express themselves and evolve. An ethic is far more than a set of practices applicable to only one sphere of activity. Therefore, the sustainability ethic should inform not only our relationship to the environment but to all aspects of life and society. Nature works therefore it is necessary to understand and apply ecological principles in all spheres. Justice and equitable access to essential resources (clean air, water, food, shelter, education, health service etc.) is an inalienable right for all regardless of sex, social and economic status to act locally and think globally. Quality is more important than quantity, conservation than consumerism as within so without it is important to cultivate a life-enhancing inner perspective.

The act of wise living involves four steps : plant purposefully, prepare prayerfully, proceed positively and pursue persistently.

Mental setbacks are hinder to cope with than the physical because it makes people ineffective. They operate from the I "cant" rather than I "can" they operate from scarcity rather than abundance. They are rooted in poverty consciousness rather than in prosperity we have to learn the art of coming from abundance rather than from scarcity. Creativity happens in this space. In the international field, new concepts are emerging in the wake of the end of the cold war and advances in technology. Satellite systems that operate from low earth orbits are being planned with the prospects of providing mobile and communication links world-wide through hand-held and other portable terminals. Other development include the testing of single stage-to-orckets, the use of imagining radar to penetrate

- Community mobilisation networking in health and sanitation for project related to welfare and development of children activities of national rural development society.
- Specific objective to organise support services to help urban slum and street children in fulfilment of his/her basic needs such as non formal education, health care, recreation to provide facilities for skill acquisition and vocational training to help and support self-help projects run by children themselves to organise children for collective action in various cooperatives, credit union, child worker, trade union.
- Organise ongoing documentation of the process of the programme, research studies on related issues that would have the direct bearing on policy formulation and programme refinement with the participatory research so that children can be involved in identifying issues and problems data collection and analysis in support to concretising and organising the children.

Approach: Vehicle student community. A term for reaching out to street children who have little or no family support can present a special problem of constraint abuse and exploitation.

- Building of contacts, offering of children, skills and sensitivity on the part of adults.
- Establishing a trusting relations based on equity and respect for the key objectives.

- Children participation in planning most of their activities.
- In the fulfilment of her/her basic needs such as :
  - (a) Non formal education' health care.
  - (b) Recreation.
  - (c) To help and protect them from the worse access of exploitation.
  - (d) To provide facilities for skill acquisition and vocational training
  - (e) To help and support self-help projects run by children themselves.
  - (f) To organise children for collective action with the feeling that it is their programme and therefore they have to make a success.
  - (g) To organise the core of programme for reigning interventions and in the process of organising children : to take a rural decision for needed compromise for alternative education for the children who have never been to schools.
  - (h) Involvement of educators at times suitable for our children to be involved in designing the curriculum and teaching/learning material to understand the realities in which they live and thereby become sensitive and relevant in their interaction with children.

CENTRE FOR HUMAN ECOLOGY AT INSTITUTE OF HOME ECONOMICS

With the new holistic challenges community based convergent services for the development of women and children meeting at the community level.

- Development programme to encourage flexibility in service approach, more relevant to the needs of women and children meeting at the community level.

University of Delhi Course of Reading for

- B.Sc Nursing
- B.Sc (Hons) Electronics
- B.Sc (Hons) Physics
- B.Com. (Hons) Mathematics
- B.Sc. (Hons) Mathematics
- B.Sc. (Hons) Statistics
- B.Sc. (Hons) Zoology
- B.Sc. (Hons) Computer Science
- B.Sc. (G) Group A — Physics, Chemistry and Mathematics
- B.Sc. (G) Group B — Chemistry, Botany and Zoology

Additional Courses

- B.Sc Agriculture
- B.Sc Horticulture
- B.Sc (Fishery)/BFSc.
- B.Sc Forestry
- B.Sc Sericulture
- B.Tec (DT)/B.Sc (DT)
- B.Tec (AE)
- B.Sc (Food Science and Technology)
- B.Sc (B&C)
- BVSc & AH.

B.Sc (Home Science) in collaboration with 20 Home Science Institutions — 4-year degree course after 10+2 in any sciences stream having Physics, Chemistry as compulsory subject.

In view of changing complexion of agricultural education

a need was felt to redefine the position of Home Science education and thereby the entire programme of Home Science has been restructured and made it relevant to the need of skill oriented training for entrepreneur development in diverse aspect for women technological empowerment.

The revised curriculum of undergraduate programme includes :

- The four-year programme would be 2+2 *i.e.,* core courses and Home Science course to be offered during the first 2 years and professional elective courses to next two years. Further Rural/urban slum, Home Science work experience and implant training would be of one semester during which student will get stipend.
- Professional elective in 5 major disciplines of Home Science are as under :
    1. Human development and Family studies (organisation and management of early childhood programme and special education).
    2. Clothing and Textile : (Apparel designing and Textile designing).
    3. Home Science Extension Education (Journalism and mass communication, distance education and information technology).
    4. Family Resource Management: (Interior Designing and Institutional house keeping).
    5. Food Science and Nutrition (Post harvest technology).
- B.Sc Hons — Botany courses
- B.Sc (H) Chemistry
- B.Sc (Gen) Anthropology
- B.Sc (Hons) Geology

- Bachelor of Dairy Technology is a 4-year degree programme after 10+2 in Physics, Chemistry and Mathematics. The course is offered in 12 institutions including National Dairy Research Institute, Karnal under ICAR-SAU Systems.

B.Sc Course Syllabus : Revision with the Changing Needs of the Students

The University of Delhi offers courses in information technology, management and other professional streams for introduction of component of vocational courses in BA courses according to the University act enacted by Parliament; the AC shall be the academic body of the university and be responsible for maintaining the standards of institutions, education and examination within the University. The academic agenda to voice the potential for excellence in search for partnership for quality research for carrying out knowledge based research and its application in B.Sc.

For evaluation to tap the strength of DU the applied science departments, leading centres of in the field of genetics, micro biology, and bio physics for the revision towards the courses with the changing needs and to act as academic body of the university.

Pre-Service

1. M.Sc Human Ecology, Biodiversity, Biotechnology and Environment Management

   Duration : 2 yrs.

   Collaboration with college of Human Ecology, Michigan

   State University, East Lansing, Michigan.
2. M.Sc in Women Agriculture and Rural Extension Management.

   Duration : 1 yr.

3. Modification of B.Ed and M.Ed courses

   Duration : 1 yr.

   Collaboration with NCERT and Department of Education, Government of India.

In-Service

1. Course on Women Agriculture, Rural Extension and Biodiversity and Biotechnology.

   Duration : 3 Months; 1 yr. Tailor made programmes.

COURSES UNDER FORMULATION AND IMPLEMENTATION

(Research Designed and Methodology)

Programme/Activities Proposed

- Continuing education courses for the university group.
- Adult Extension Education for those eligible for university based courses Research.

Role and functions of the Department of Adult Continuing extension, education and field outreach.

Catalyst Role

- Acting as focal agency in the University system.
- Serving as technical resource centre for universities community activities.
- Assessing the need of the community.
- Developing curriculum and multidisciplinary University programmes, involving faculty students from various disciplines.
- Stimulating other departments of the University to undertake similar activities with respect to their discipline for continuing education of graduates, extension education and field outreach.

Teaching, Training and Research for socially disadvantaged group

- Under the framework of women participation in management, integration of services, at an institution — to provide feedback guide implementation — to improve quality of life in farm, off-farm and non-farm sector for human resource development.
- Development with special reference to tribal women through the strategy which include social empowerment, education and development.

A project proposal entitled "Research and Training in on-farm, off-farm and non-farm sectors for human resources development with special reference to tribal women."

- Teaching programmes/course in adult and continuing education.
- Conducting need based continuing education courses not undertaken by other departments of the university.
- Conducting activities/programmes for upgrading knowledge skills or acquiring new skills short-term diploma certificates programmes.
- Training short-term aimed at various groups is skill income generation, entrepreneurship development family life education, Para legal training for grass-root workers/activities.
- Community outreach activities — responsibility to reach out to society, specific disadvantaged groups, *e.g.* bonded labour, child workers, urban slum and villages.

PROGRAMMES

- Vocational/Career oriented programmes.

- Empowering people at different socio-economic and educational levels with marketable vocational skills, which are appropriate.
- Participation in literacy, post literacy, continuing education under the ground level model.
- Evaluation as per university norms. Collaborating and Networking
- Networking with government departments and other agencies of the country.
- International collaborations — to implement the programmes for higher education and to draw the programmes of collaboration by the participating institute — for linking higher education in the priority areas of environment, population education and science and technology and gender issues.

Documentation particularly of Field Experience to Enrich Theory and dissemination of Information :

- Preparing material
- Disseminating information
- Use of computers and internet-Publications Monitoring and Evaluation
- Monitoring and Evaluating the Department's activities as well as ongoing extension in the university.
- Reporting to Nodal Centre/University.

Education and Outreach Technical Programme at Centre for Human Ecology

- Two years postgraduate programmes in human ecology, Bio-diversity, and environment, Bio-technology.
- Pre-service — Human Ecology.
- One year (In-service, pre-service) programme for

development in human ecology Bio-diversity and environment, Bio-technology.

- Modification of B.Ed, M.Ed courses. In-Service Courses
- Three months general management programmes in women agriculture rural extension and life sciences related certificate courses.
- Courses on women agriculture and rural extension.
- Courses and training programmes on agricultural education and life sciences-teacher's certificate courses.

Top Down Approach

One of the characteristics of the structural transformation of women in agriculture is the prevalence of substantial women labour force-especially those belonging to the backward groups. Such as scheduled castes women ability to make agricultural policy is limited. Indian women has religious sanctions reflected in various religious scripture like Manu Smriti, so much so many of their invisible arduous economic activities in agriculture go unnoticed and unaccounted.

Foreign universities for: Development and modification of course curricula at postgraduate and undergraduate level.

Overseas training: Education technology for outreach training programmes : collaboration with the universities of USA.

Texas A & M University: To develop the human resources; faculty exchange for institutional capacity building in the areas of evaluation methodology; ecosystems; meat processing technology; skill development for Agribusiness education.

Collaboration with ISNAR for research training in the various disciplines of agriculture and management of research, joint collaborative projects and study visit in respect of scientist and scholar for international linkages for Human Resource Development with special reference to Agriculture and Rural Extension and other institutions for training on pre-service and in-service graduates.

Key Issues

To help people, help themselves through the practical application of knowledge and resources to improve their quality of life and that of future generations.

Objectives

- To strengthen and to achieve the goal of sustainable development.
- To encourage the environment ethics at both formal and non-formal education.
- Use of media in promoting environmental and development awareness.
- To provide a support network at international and national local level.
- To provide data basis on programmes, projects that created a paradigm shift towards more widespread intellectual voices in higher education.
- Technical programmers will include : Ph.D in Human Ecology, M.Sc in Human Ecology, Biodiversity Biotechnology and Environment Management, M.Sc in Women Agriculture and Rural Extension Management; Modification of B.Ed and M.Ed courses.

CHAPTER 6

Empowerment of Women in Human Ecology

As the century begins, natural resources are under increasing pressure, threatening public health and development. Water shortage, soil exhaustion, loss of forests, air water pollution, and degradation of coastline afflict many areas. As the world population grows, improving living standards without destroying the environment is a global challenge.

Women have unique and valuable perspective to bear upon the application of science and technology to development. Women researchers can play a key role to pursue the high objectives of the collective endeavour jointly with men to over come the barriers of discrimination the impede the health education and carrier of women also the critical challenges on the growing gap between the science rich countries of the north and the science poor countries of south in the production and use of scientific and technological knowledge.

To generate facilities to be used by the scientists industries and students all over the country for the multifarious activities in the country. Financial assistance to, Post Graduate, post doctoral, certificate courses, diploma courses in biotechnology and allied fields of Human Ecology National and International associate ships for research and training in leading research laboratories in the country and abroad, short term training courses, to train mid carrier scientists.

Training Programmes

To pursue post graduate training leader to a doctorate degree at centers of excellence in the country and out side own country. The specific aims of the schemes are:

1. To improve access to educational and training opportunity for young talented women graduates.
2. To increase scientific productivity and creativity

For the most part, the above suggestions depend on a traditional model describing the research, policy and programme relationship in which research results are first created and their communicated from researchers to the potential users. The communication may be face to face or may occur in written or visual form. An intermediary acting on behalf of the researchers, such as policy institution may break the research results, or a professional association engaged lobying. "Basic" research findings may also be transformed into a technological application, which is pass on to practitioners. In addition policy maker and practitioners are associated with Government, and therefore the main interface is sought with Government personnel.

The traditional way of thinking about research and its practical consequences have served characteristics that should be made explicit. First the researchers and the user are always separate. Second the following from the first, knowledge is always transferred from one person to another. Third, research results are first arrived at, then disseminated (perhaps after being repackaged or turned into technology), when judging the success of transfer of knowledge to action, there is tendency also to associated specific pieces of research or specific outcomes of research with specific policies or action into world of policy and practice.

The traditional way of approaching to relationship between research and its use into practice is not wrong. Such interface can occur and they can and should be fostered. However, this view is limiting and in my opinion, probably does not represent the principal way in which research gets converted to action. What are the alternative conceptions and what do they imply? These are the use of media to research the public in corporating researches into the evaluation of ongoing programmes and encouraging the students to become involved in research with policy orientation. Indeed, the difficulty of making these more direct connections and of building the desired partnership was illustrated by the failure of many invited individuals from the policy and programming side to participate in the symposium. The only interface for researchers who would like to see their research results translated into action is with governments it recognises that research can be used directly by the public and can be empower. But less often recognised, reason for taking public limited to necessarily to a literate public in these cases as an audience is that, in democracies, the public in these cases as an audience is that, in democracies, the public put pressure on their government to change policies as seems to be the case at present. In this case the journalist and proper writer and even the television producer or actor may become the most important allies of the researcher, an indirect inter face between research and practice. Directing research results to public is an important option for researchers, but this approach barely breaks away from the traditional way of thinking about the research — practice nexus. It avoids the leniency to associate specific research findings with specific changes in policy and practice by looking beyond those in governments who set policy and plan programme. However, the approach continues to separate researcher from user and is linear in conception. In this non-linear view, the dissemination and use of knowledge begins to occur with the conceptualisation of a research project. It occurs over the course of the research process. It is embodied in people who carry out research and who then use the technology without having the knowledge, without having to transfer what was learned to others.

In this more radical view, we are led to think as much about who formulates and carries out research and about the specific content of the research. We are led to the idea of participatory research; along side the academic purpose, become to change the attitude and behaviour of the research/ practitioner.

Involving graduate students in research whereby they will use what they have learned in the course of the research, is the most obvious case fitting the model. But it is far from being the only case. For instance, there are situations in which knowledge acquired in themselves move into policy or programme making positions or because practitioners are incorporated into research with the idea that the research is directed towards informing their own work.

Attempts to incorporate practitioners directly into research becomes important incorporating researchers into practice. One can imagine, for instance, cases of classroom teachers or early childhood promoters who are involved in continuing education or training in which they take their own classroom as the basis for research. It may reflect a desire to impart the truth discovered in previous research and which deserves to be transmitted. It may effect a desire to avoid reinvestigating the wheel. Even though a case can be made for the efficiency of such reinvention because it increases the chances that the new wheel will actually be used. Given the proper atmospheres and methodologies linking action to reflection such participatory research can overcome the possible problems of bias in observation can be done without sacrificing rigour and can lead to immediate use of research results. Incorporating directly into research is not a realistic, involving teachers in research is to place the students in internships in government offices, where policies are made and programmes are carried out. These study opportunities could be planned around projects directly related to their work and around research that would feed into their work. The reader will certainly be able to think of others feasible combinations that would bring the researchers and user back to face between research policy and programming.

Making community policy to make market based mechanism to address climate change and promote transfer of finance and climate friendly technology to developing countries.

Established with contribution from government and private sectors to operate and to improve environmental pursuing profits. While a vibrant and growing agricultural sector is vital for reducing poverty agriculture alone is insufficient to solve action oriented phase the policy framework and a good rural strategy are critical, sustained commitment to rural development is important. Data availability is a serious problem.

A doubling of food production to feed a extra 2 billion people by 2025 most of them in developing country will require new and improved agricultural technologies in promoting policies, indigenous people, and cultural property has been improving. Promoting increased participation in civil society in natural level policymaking is more responsive and transparent.

Community driver approaches to development — giving local organisations more say — can make resource allocation more responsive to the need of poor and increase of power of poor community to interact with government, the private sector and civil society in planning and implementing their own development programmes with similar efforts envisaged to disseminate information on legal and procurement matter. Training programmes for in-service community to promote best practice and piloting of initiatives in conflict prevention.

Cultural identity is an essential part of empowering communities to take change of their own destinies from tourism to restoration, investments in cultural heritage promote labour intensive economic activities that generate wealth and income.

GLOBALISATION WITH A HUMAN FACE

The real wealth of a nation is its people. And the purpose of development is to create an enabling environment for people to enjoy long, healthy and creative lives. This simple but powerful truth is too often forgotten in the pursuit of material and financial wealth.

Globalisation is now new, but the present era has distinctive features. Shrinking space, shrinking time and disappearing borders are linking people's lives more deeply, more intensely, more immediately than ever before. Globalisation offers great opportunities for human advance but only with stronger governance.

This era of globalisation is opening many opportunities for million of people around the world. Increased trade, new technologies, foreign investments, expanding media and internet connections are fuelling economic growth and human advance. All this offers enormous potential to eradicate poverty in the 21st century — to continue the unprecedented progress in the 20th century. We have more wealth and technology — and more commitment to a global community than ever before.

Global markets, global technology, global ideas and global solidarity can enrich the lives of people everywhere, greatly expanding their choices. The growing interdependence of people's lives calls for shared values and a shared commitment to the human development of all people. The challenges is to find the rules and institutions for stronger governance — local, national, regional and global markets and completion, but also to provide enough space for human, community and environmental resources to ensure that globalisation works.

(a) Entrepreneurial Opportunity in Agriculture

Horticulture, Vegetable, Floriculture, Mushroom cultivation, Seed Production, Medicinal and Aromatic Plant production foods, biscuits, confectionary (including cocoa processing and chocolate making), malt extract, protein isolate high protein food, weaning food and extruded food products (including other ready-to-eat foods).

Beer, including non-alcoholic beer. Alcoholic drinks from non-molasses base. Aerated waters/soft drinks and other processed foods. Specialised packaging for food processing industries. Establishment and servicing of the development councils for food processing industries.

(b) Post Harvest Technology for Value Addition and Nutrition

- Fruits and vegetable processing industry including freezing and dehydration :
  - — Food grain milling industry
  - — Consumer food industry
  - — Bakery, cocoa products, soft drinks, beer and alcoholic drinks, fruit and vegetable.
- Traditional methods of processing cereals, pulses and grains and modern appropriate techniques and reforms.
- Fortification of cereals/cereal products for enhancing the nutritional level of our population, especially women and children.
- Setting up of mobile fruit and vegetable processing unit.
- Person-power development for entrepreneurship and transfer of technology for processing of food products, production cum training centres.

(c) Agro-Based Enterprises

- Introduction of innovative protein rich items with

special reference to-dairy, poultry, meat, mushroom and yeast.

- Community food programmes, supplementary feeding programmes, school lunch programme.
- Testing and development of new food product for space exploration, novel food products.

Indian Council of Agricultural Research

The ICAR has been the facilitator of Green, White and Blue Revolutions. The technologies generated by the scientists had been the cornerstones of our past successes. To achieve the twin national objectives of poverty alleviation and welfare of the disadvantaged and weaker sections of the society, it has now become imperative to increase agricultural productivity, profitability, and sustainability through judicious and more integrated use of our natural resources. However, our production of agri-horticultural crops has secured a prestigious position within the century.

The agricultural sector with its significant share in GDP *plays a significant role in the employment* generation especially in the rural sector. It has significant potential as a net foreign exchange earner.

The main approach of the government policy has been to control trade in a manner to ensure adequate availability of essential food items to consumers at reasonable process and to protect farmers from foreign competition.

Agricultural Extension is aimed at promoting agricultural development by providing farmers with information and training on continuous basis regarding improved production technologies and their adoption.

The extension programmes and activities of the directorate are specifically planned and implemented in the following four specific sectors :

- — Extension Management.
- — Extension Training
- — Farm Information
- — Farm Women Development Programme.

The Ministry of Food Processing

The Ministry of Food Processing Industries was set up to give an impetus to the development of food processing industries in the country. A strong and effective food processing sector plays a significant role in diversification and commercialisation of agriculture, improves value addition of the agricultural produce, generates employment, enhances income of farmers. The Ministry is concerned with the formulation and implementation of the policies and plans for the food processing industries within the overall national priorities and objectives like.

1. Policy Support

(a) Formulation and implementation of policies for food processing industries within overall national priorities and objectives.

(b) Facilitating the creation of a conducive policy environment for healthy growth of the food processing sector.

(c) Promoting rationalisation of tariff and duties in relation to food processing sector.

2. *Development*

(a) Assistance under various plan schemes.

(b) Widening the R&D base in food processing by involvement of various R&D institutes and support to various R&D activities relating to development of product, process and packaging with special emphasis on traditional technologies.

(c) Human Resource Development both for

entrepreneurs as well as the workers engaged in the food processing industry by upgradation of their skills.

(d) Assistance for setting up analytical and testing laboratories, active participation in the laying down of food standards as well as their harmonisation with international standards.

3. Promotional

Assistance for organisation of workshops, seminars, exhibitions and fairs etc.

Frontiers of knowledge are henceforth bound to expand unimaginably and new researchers will oblige humanities, societies, technologies and fine arts to arrive at new equations and new combinations. Development in communication, information and technology will open new and cost effective approaches for enhancing the reach of higher education to meet the demands of fast changing nature of employment.

India has been in the forefront of all global initiative that have communicated the philosophy of *Human Ecology*. The scientific expertise to increase the relevance of higher education by making courses in use career oriented. To enhance empowerment in human resources with special emphasis on education the disciplines of agribusiness, bio-diversity and environment, biotechnology, non-conventional energy system like a perspective of higher education for community empowerment. To meet the challenges imposed by new economic and social order, and improve the quality of life to make a positive impact on the immediate society to which they belong. Adequate field experience in academic programmes coupled with practical work experience combined with outstanding teaching and strong foundation in applied and social sciences which will provide graduate students with the vision on the study of behavioural aspects implied with the interrelationship of the biotic components with the practical application.

Community resource management concerns for the management of resources for the development of needs of the family and community for social equity and people's participation in a tree interactive process. Large number of NGO's and Voluntary agencies have now centred the value education in India. Some of them have evolved innovative programmes.

Home science in reality is deeply and closely related to life. A model home science curriculum would, therefore, are to cover all such factors fields, and interests which affects a person's development, his life, in the family and in the community: A change to meet the challenges and opportunities of today's higher education centre. Today higher education enterprise, an immensely broad based discipline to determine our success or failure in overcoming environmental challenges and achieving sustainable development. Cities and towns provide enormous, untapped opportunities to solve environmental challenges, they must and can pioneer new approaches to sustainable development and community management.

Earth is the laboratory where biological and physical processes are experimented. An endeavour to improve the quality of life warrants a thorough understanding of various earth system processes. The 21st century in an era of accelerated development in all activities of life conceivable. Any attempt to satiate the development urge, neglecting earth, will boomerang and will set in stumbling blocks across our path to progress. The task ahead for planning and development is to comprehend the mother earth in its totality, involving land, water and atmosphere to allow sustainable life possible.

Man is an important element of the environmental complex. His activities, growing population, industrial and urban settlement, social religious and economic setups are posing newer ecological problems. Understanding his ecological role the anthropologists, sociologists, psychologists, economists, demographers supply data to persons working on human ecology. To be acquainted with various disciplines of physical and biological sciences in order to get integrated picture of the environmental complex in relation to the organic world. In order to quantify his data an ecologist has to collect information, which could be subjected to mathematical formulation for precise communication to others working in the field. Indian culture is deeply rooted in two different but intricate traditions. In India awakening has begun. More and more of the scientists, artists, scholars have started looking into their rich traditions, for large synthesis of knowledge. It has to collaborate in bringing out concerted action for knowledge, universal upliftment and lasting peace and unity. For humanity to successfully meet the evolutionary and revolutionary challenges of contemporary advancement — great cultural achievements of the past must be revised and enriched to bring about a new type of humanity. A society marked by integrated power of physical, emotional, dynamic, intellectual, clinical, aesthetic and spiritual potentialities. vocational and professional elements, which need to be exploited to the fullest extent in future educational needs.

Professional courses would provide wide spectrum of experience to graduating students hence sufficient weightage have to be given to make students professions and befitted in development departments for the effective enterprise development. We have to be at risk taking and innovative in view of dynamic changes of global liberalisation and marketing strategies and knowledge that improves daily lives of current and future generations.

To develop proficiency in students for planning, organizing, and evaluating rural development programmes especially programmes for youth and women to be supported by fieldwork and field projects examining the family as a significant ecosystem.

Management programmes explores design and function in conjuction with technology user satisfaction and perception.

The university community should make special effort to increase the relevance of higher education by making the courses carrier oriented by developing interdisciplinary knowledge and skills for research, extension programmes to outreach the communities. It must empower human resource with special emphasis on educating the disciplines of Agribusiness, Biodiversity and Environment, Biotechnology, Non Conventional Energy System, to raise unified field of *Human Ecology* for Community empowerment.

A living organism and environment surrounding it cannot be separated from each other. The system arising from the interaction of a biological community with its non-living surroundings is called ecosystem as an ecological unit that has both structure and function. The structure includes an analysis of biotic communities living in a habitat and the physical features of the environment, including edaphic factors, nutrition, and climatic conditions.

Man's relationship with his environment now occupies a major place among the problems. Therefore, it is necessary to demonstrate the scientific programmes in a way towards meeting the safe and sustainable future to mankind.

To respond to human needs the main thrust will be directed towards the activities which are socially beneficial and economically viable; like farm, off-farm and non-farm sectors.

The national agricultural technology project has made stride under three major components :

1. Agro-ecosystem research,

2. Innovation in technology dissemination, and
3. Organisation and management system. ·

Let us be set up for balancing higher education for community service :

- For the hope of a better and safe future needed for the management of human and environment in improve people's life and environment in the view of rapid technological advancement and community belonging to the poorest of the poor families.
- Earth eco-system research: To mobilise community support in understanding, promoting and enabling better child care through education.
- To provide supportive services through education, women's development programmes such as safe drinking water, environmental sanitation, and preschool education below 6 years.
- Nutrition and health education by the community the referral services in expectant and nursing mothers, and women in age group of 15 to 45 years.
- For institution strengthening and linkages for research capacity building in collaborative programmes in research and training.
- To promote participation in education to bring in to sharp focus the central role of human development, in to poverty education.
- To promote behaviour studies with practical application of knowledge across the domains of research, outreach and international programmes.

Institutionalisation of Extension Curriculum

The colleges have to become a catalyst in the future learning society, a centre of education and development for the students and the community through both formal and non-formal means.

The students would use the community as social laboratory for their practical, moral and attitudinal education and learn by working in and serving the community.

The extension activities be incorporated in the undergraduate courses, in foundation courses, applied courses, community service, project work, and in basic or core courses.

Institutionalisation of extension needs academic acceptance which is automatically ensured when the activities enter at a stage of studies and research which enlarges our understanding and contributes to knowledge. Extension activities can enter into research through :

- Project work or field-based dissertation at undergraduate and post-graduate levels.
- Post-graduate courses with research component related to extension activities in the form of case studies.
- M.Phil, and Ph.D. as well as post-doctoral programmes.

It is essential to transform some selected colleges into Community Colleges. They should be given complete academic autonomy for innovations and experimentation.

Radio, T.V., Video-Audio tapes, VCR, VBCP, etc. are the modern electronic communication media that are reaching slowly every village and house. The access to these equipment should be available to the disadvantaged regions and communities through Community Education Centres with active participation of the community itself. Colleges can play a great role in organising and maintaining such centres and make them very effective centres of extensions.

Universities and the Adult Education Programme

It is within the ability and structural conduciveness of the colleges and universities to assume effectively the role of resource centres for adult education for research, orientation, material development, and evaluation, etc. The colleges are best suited to be developed as local resource centres for adult education as they are the knowledge centres with community of scholars and students pursuing knowledge in different discipline For post-literacy and continuing education programmes, the colleges and universities are the most appropriate agencies to be involved. Colleges and universities can also be effectively used.

Indian corporate circle in the early 70s, it gained popularity in the country only when the Government of India constituted the Ministry of Human Resource Development at the centre. It was realized, for the first time, both at the macro and micro operations that the development of the country or organization depended to a greater extend on the development of human resource of different types rather than the development of material resources such as the land and building, capital, machine, material, technology etc., and that the integration of the group goals with the national goals and employees; goals with the organizational goals essential ingredients for overall growth and development. Since then, several organizations belonging to the private, public and joint sectors of the country have either started new HRD departments or appointed HRD managers or taken initiative to strengthen their personnel departments to look after the HRD functions. In nutshell, the HRD movement has taken off in the country.

Present Scenario

The HRD movement, which began in the country during the 80s of the current century, has remained lop-sided that is, confined to the managerial personnel only even after the lapse of more than 25 years. The HRD of workers is deliberately overlooked. Advancing on the traditional path of Marxism, the trade union organizations of the country have remained passive and mostly slient on the unions role in educating the workers of HRD. The subjects covers, so far, under the grants-in-aid programmes to trade unions/other institutions of the Central Board of Workers' Education are mostly legal or economic and not developmental. The reason for the total apathy of the trade union leaders towards workers' education for HRD is, perhaps, the fear that their leadership may be in danger if a new class of contented, satisfied, self-dependent and assertive workers looking after their own interests emerges out of the HRD-oriented educational programmes. The workers may even ask for their participation in the union affairs and this will not be in the interest of the ageing and retired trade union activities heading the Trade Union Movement of the country. Moreover, these trade union leaders do not want to assume the collaborative role and want to confine with the traditional roles as this practice may reduce their bargaining power and shift the workers' loyality from unions to managements. The relegation of workers affairs to the corporate Industrial Relations Department having no coordination with the HRD Department shows the aversion of the corporate managements towards the HRD education for workers. The effects of any educational and developmental efforts directed on a particular group of employees and overlooking altogether the rank and file comprising the majority of the total human assets of any organization are bound to be marginal and half-hearted from the viewpoint of organizational growth and development and as such undesirable.

Restructuring and Productivity

The world is in transition from the industry-based and regional or national based society of 19-20th century to a knowledge-based and 'one world one village' or global society in the 21st century. This is the advent of the information technology era that is due to the convergence of the computer, communication and electronic technologies. In the 21st century, knowledge will be the key and the fundamental sources of wealth will be knowledge and information rather than raw materials and labour.

It is particularly strong in four leading sectors : information and communication technologies, intellectual property-patents, brand names, advertising and financial services databases and recreational services; and biotechnology. It is often said if we can transport lots of bits so easily and so quickly and so economically, there is no need to transport raw materials and physical labour.

The mantra of getting competitive edge in the age of liberalization and globalization is Lead of Follow. Therefore, going for 'lead' is the best mantra of the present days competitive advantages. Poor countries like India, have thus to go for a 'lead' through improved human resources generation in a process of evolution, which shall be innovative and rapid. Till today, human generation is not done at factory but at the institutions of higher learning and research like universities, engineering and medical colleges/institutes, etc. The speculation of 'self-designing beings' who would continue to improve themselves at an ever increasing rate. Under such situations the reduced budget allocation for higher education implemented in recent past in many poor countries is not beyond the preview of questions and criticism.

The Case of India

Since 1992, India has taken part in the liberalization, privatization and globalization process. So India needs to improve human resources particularly in technical/higher education and research. But in international standing of higher education and research, not only India's position is poor but also it is becoming poorer day by day. Irony is that this picture has emerged after India's taking part in liberalization process, whereas this should have been be the other way round. There are different parameters to see the position of human resources, like Human Resources Index defined by the UNO, etc. For the purpose of higher education and research, we may analyze data based on other more appropriate parameters.

It is amply clear that India is not following the correct path to become a leader in the world of globalization. In poor countries and, therefore, in India also, it is often assumed that higher education is not appropriate at the cost of other social infrastructure like basic education, health, etc. But we must analyze whether higher education is really costly in India and if so what are the reasons for that and must find path to abnegate those reasons. Higher education in India is costly because of the following reasons :

1. India, and for that matter most or all of the poor countries, education system and structure are copied or borrowed from advanced countries. We have no innovative system and structure of our own to meet our environment and requirements.
2. Investment return on higher education in poor countries including India is low.
3. Imbalance and improper fund allocation to the institutes.

Investment Return on Higher Education

It is often said that the investment return on higher education is less or marginal. The marginal rates for the college and university in India are lower that the returns for below college level studies. Therefore, more investments and higher subsidies on the education below college level would be more beneficial for both the individual and the society than that on higher education. But in this study only individual income was considered for the calculation of return. In case of higher education more emphasis should be given to the national income than the individual income. For example, an engineer's monthly salary is not the only return, his service in terms of production in the factory, development of techniques and system (that may be assumed as income of nation through his service) are the major returns.

The main reasons for low investment return on higher education are (a) brain drain, and (b) non-involvement of professional persons in the policy farming of even project specific matters.

The gravity of the problem caused by brain-drain shall minimize if people migrating abroad shall even marginally invest in nation building. Nowadays, NRIs are participating in the national projects and developments. This is encouraging at the same time, we must do something at least to reduce. Higher perks and pay and freedom in work place of progressional persons are the major issues which need to be considered seriously to reduce brain-drain.

Any move to limit higher education and research by any means shall be counterproductive for growth and prosperity of the nation. The argument that poor countries should not and cannot bear the high cost of higher education, and that too at the expenses of elementary education and basic health, etc., is good to hear in the first instance.

Criteria for distribution of funds to the institutes of higher learning and research by a parameter of productivity of the institutes rather than their products and image, etc., has also been proposed. It is believed that suggestions made in here in conformity with the tenet 'think globally act locally' which is often taken as the way of going with liberalization. Reducing higher education in poor countries shall be first suicidal step in the age of open economy and information revolution.

The proper analysis of this argument and whether higher education is really costly and if so what are the reasons behind that need to be examined before taking a decision.

Following are the main thrust in the Nineth Plan guidelines

of UGC for centres/departments of Adult Continuing Education and Extension and field outreach :

1. In the Ninth Plan, every university should establish a centre/department of Adult Continuing Education and Extension. The adult continuing education and outreach activities should become an integral part of all departments and constituents of the university through the optimum involvement of teachers and students. The universities need to give a statutory status to the departments/centres for Adult Continuing Education and Extension, if needed even by amending the University Acts and Statutes. The department/centre will have the same status as any other academic/ teaching department of the university with core faculty eligible for representation on all the university bodies such as senate, academic council, board of studies, etc.

Adult Continuing Education and Extension during the Nineth Plan are the following :

- Undergraduate and postgraduate level courses in adult and continuing education/non-formal education.
- Certificate/diploma courses in adult education.
- Projects related to extension/field outreach and foundation courses.
- Research/Documentation/Publication. Training programmes for students/community/ teachers.

The language with experience of children was extended to upper primary and secondary stage as part of general education. The environmental concept problems and introduction of social and environmental studies provided teachers with a curricular area in which the need and interest of children could be met through a focus on the local environment. Students must be given the opportunity to develop the sense of ownership, and empowerment so that they are fully invested in an environmental sense and motivated to become responsible active citizens.

Yeshpal Committee Report 1993 strongly recommended Gandhian approach to learning. Many other institutions in different parts of the country use different approaches and methodologies with same and results. What runs through them all is the thread of spirituality and ecological thinking. All these institutions is still value education through course work as well as practices. It would be infect appropriate to describe the institutional framework for training and research in sociology, which as emerged after independence. Sociology in India is largely a discipline of borrowed concepts and methods derived from high prestige centres of learning in affluent wet especially in the USA and UK. This has resulted in chasing high prestige models into quick sand of Psendo-intellection. Sociologists have still not related themselves directly to the people and their problems and still reveling in counter productive intellectualism. Our sociology does not address itself to the living concern of today and tomorrow. As a result it is not able to contribute meaningfully towards resolving many dilemmas of development.

The concept of human resource system therefore assumes that human being is great asset in the organization. They are not merely necessarily evils to be reckoned with but they can contribute a great deal to the achievement of organizational as an asset with the unlimited potential in he concept of Human Resource Systems. The study of people at most is generally referred to as the study of organizational behaviour. It is the systematic study of the actions and attitude that people exhibit with in organization. The field of organizational behaviour (OB) is based on large number of systematically designed research studies. An organization is a formal structure of planned coordination involving two or more people in order to achieve in common goal.

Contributing Disciplines

Organizational behaviour is applied behaviour science and as a result, is built upon. Contributions from several behaviours discipline. The predominant are psychology, sociology, social psychology, anthropology and political science. Psychology's contribution has been mainly at individual or micro level of analysis, whereas the latter disciplines have contributed to our understanding of macro concepts-group processes and organizational behaviour. The psychology explains or some times changes the behaviour of humans and other animals. The goals of human behaviour studies are concerned with developing people's skills, help to explain, predict and control human behaviour. The human behaviour studies after technologies that facilitate the control of people infect. Whether these technologies should be used in organization becomes ethical question are should be aware, that the control objectives are frequently seen by managers as the most valuable contribution that human behaviour makes towards effectiveness on the jobs. Today's managers understand that the success of any effort at improving quality and productivity must include their employees. These employees will only be major force in changing out changes but increasingly will actively participate in planning other changes.

Improving People's Skill

The relevant theory and concepts that can help one, plain and predicts the behaviour of people. These are variety of ways to motivate people, how to be better communicator and how to create more effective team to be used in the job.

Motivating the Workforce

Reconstituted into job requiring considerable higher technical skills or taking workers in other countries that will do the same work for a fraction of the wages. In this situation employee tends to perform either low skilled jobs or higher skilled jobs that means to maintain a middle class or upper class life style. This situation leads to a major challenge for mangers. How to motivate who are making very low wage and have very little opportunity to significantly increase their pay either in current or trough promotion.

System Development and Research

Various systems for human resource systems need to be continuously designed, tested and reviewed. Data being collected also need to be analyzed to give dues to the developing interventions. Development of human resource system can be conceived a system with inter linkages amongst its various components. The central concern of various components of HRS seems to be job. Job is defined in terms of critical attributes, background characteristics necessary like education and training and experience person has before he takes up the job we get training needs out of the critical attributes which also contribute to the concept of career planning of education and training. If we further expand we get into several new directions. The concept of human resource management is an approach to the management of the people. The behavioural science movement made two useful contributions to HRM.

Organization development movement : the organizational development (OD) movement advocated the implementation of programmes designed to improve the effectiveness with which organization functions and responds to change, with particular emphasis on how people carry out their work and interest with one another. The total approach to organizational behaviour exerted a strong influence on many of these who in the late 70's and early 80's began concentrate on corporate culture as a central issue in the management of human resource. Different organizations have different traditions. In some organizations personal function may already include some aspects like general administration such as general administration such special features will certainly influence the design of some aspect of HRS. The traditional factor where HRS was designed as a part of the personal function. Where HRS was introduced, administration was also put along with the department was designated human resource administration.

Challenges and Opportunities

The human behaviour studies solutions or at least some meaningful insights towards solutions. The relevant concepts and theories that can help one, plan and predict. Each organization has its own tradition. These influence the design of human, resource systems to organize activities aimed at helping individual and community. Education, labour, legislation and recreation contribute to the well-being of population.

Social Work is a professional service, based on scientific knowledge and skill in human relations which helps individuals, groups or communities to meet their basic needs, and at promoting their well being and the highest possible degree of self respect, dignity and freedom of thought and action with interfering with the same right of others.

Social security is a programme of protection provided in social legislation against sickness, unemployment, old age and disability.

Social welfare is as old as humanity itself. Helping the needy and the person in distress has been in existence particularly in all the civilization communities. From time immured. Social welfare has recently developed into a scientific programme poverty, sickness suffering, social degradation have always been known to man in long course of history of mankind, but after the industrial revolution new social problems were erased, which could not be faced by the older human institutions — family, neighbourhood and local community. In fact this was not the situation only in industrial societies particularly in the wet, but such a situation is being created in the developing countries also. Apart from the humanitarian aspect, the development of scientific knowledge provided the tools for investigating the causes of poverty, of human deficiencies and dissatisfaction with the sole object to find out a remedy for various social problems facing the society. Hence social welfare development into a scientific concept based on a scientific knowledge of the problems facing the society, particularly in free society with the object of finding out ways and means of solving these problems.

The concept of service of one's fellow men has been an integral part of Indian traditions. The raptures shared the responsibilities of meeting the needs of the individuals and groups in difficulties, the rich and the members of the general community shared the individuals and the group's difficulty. Religion institutions also played a very important part in providing social service. We come across men and women and group of persons who devote their lives to the service of helpless. The measures of goodwill and some leisure time with the industrialization and urbanization, our social problems are becoming more and more complex. There is also a growing recognition that for handling such complex social problems of social, economic and human relationship, we require cretin technical knowledge concerning human behaviour, social institutions etc.

The understanding of social relationship, social psychology and social economics has helped to understand the social problems and the ways and means of organizing social welfare services on scientific basis with the help of a tested body of knowledge. An orphan child needs more than food and clothing in children's institution. The problems of aged and infirm persons are partly social and partly psychological in nature. Therefore, the institutions of this basic human needs. There is a need for social welfare programmes like balwadis, holiday homes, youth hostels etc. which help in the prevention of occurrence of social problems. The programmes of social assistance have also to play a very important part in building up the human material. Various services like creche, orphanages, and homes for the blind, workshops of the orthopaedically handicapped persons, community welfare contract were set up by the interested citizens for the purpose of providing welfare services to the needy and the destitute.

Whereas, there has been a large measure of goodwill and dedication, there has been dearth of technical knowledge required to run various welfare services. Foreign literature was available on various social welfare services but this was not suited to the requirements of Indian condition. Attempts have been Made in certain areas of welfare, work to provide material on different kinds of social welfare service, like minimum standards on child care institutions, worked out by the Indian conference of social work, and the minimum standards for different welfare programmes by the central social welfare board etc. some useful material is also available from the reports of various committees and proceedings of conference and seminars on social legislation. All this material is not only inadequate but is not available to the social workers nib one place.

Attempts have been made in certain areas of work but this was not suited to the requirements of Indian conditions. Dedication of service towards one's fellowmen, love for charity and brotherhood existed even in times religion emphasized the values of charity philanthropy and mutual help. Indian history revert that the responsibility of assessing the individual in need was hared by the community and the rulers. During the period of King Ashoka one reads about the appointment of Gopas who were supposed to keep the records of caste, gotra, occupation births, deaths, marriage etc. the duties of Gopas were akin to modern social workers. The king took more and more responsibility towards providing social services to the public. During the early British period the impact of education and economic the reformers fought for equality of rights for women and abolition of widow re-marriage. The voluntary organization like Araya Manila Samoa, Anjuman-e-Himayat-e-Islam, Ramkrishana Mission, Theosophical society. Servants of Indian society and a large number of Christian missionaries contributed considerably to the provision of welfare services for the needy and the handicapped.

These traditions of social services were influenced by various social and economic factors. The social institutions like the joint family, The caste system and the village panchayats provided mechanism, which would meet the needs of the sick, the aged, the destitute and the handicapped members of the community. Industrialization and urbanization also changed the pattern of life. New social problems cropped up, for the solution of which the existing social institutions found themselves ineffective. Without the development of social science it beacon possible to make a systematic study if the social problems in order to solve these on a comprehensive and scientific basis. We, therefore, started moving is nonbeing laid on the application of scientific methods to the solution of social problems *i.e.* by studying the social and economic factors of the problem and acquiring special skills and techniques, in dealing with them.

Social Welfare Board : Social welfare services were brought on the political map of India 1953 with the setting up of the central social welfare as a part of First Five Year Plan. During the recent years there has been increasing realization that with a view to improving and preserving the human capital which is one of the most important factors of production of any economic development. It is necessary to provide opportunities for growth and development of the child. The social welfare field has so far been a combination of various social welfare activities without aiming at an integrated approach either to the child or to a family or to the community.

CHAPTER 7

Globalisation of Agriculture and Food Security

UGC NODAL CENTER AT JNU

(For the Faculty of JNU)

A systematic efforts for developing human resource at the grass roots level in the directions of sustainable development

FOR ESTABLISHMENT OF ASIAN CENTER FOR HUMAN ECOLOGY
FOR WOMEN AND CHILD
(UNDER PLANNING COMMISSION, GOVT OF INDIA)

PATRON

PRIME MINISTER
OF INDIA

CHAIRPERSON

STATE MINISTER DEPTT.
OF WOMEN AND CHILD

CHANCELLOR

VICE PRESIDENT
OF INDIA

VICE CHANCELLOR

PRO VICE CHANCELLOR

SCHOOLS

CENTERS

INTERNATIONAL CENTER FOR
BIODIVERSITY AND ENVIRONMENT
DELHI UNIVERSITY, SOUTH CAMPUS

*

CENTER FOR HUMAN ECOLOGY
INDIRA GANDHI OPEN UNIVERSITY

To empower a new generation of talented women to assume a leadership role in science and technology and their application in sustainable development

Nature

- The scheme to provide fellowships to young female students in and institution out side country, or choose to register as Ph.D. student in her own country and pursue part of her research at another institution under sandwich program
- Each fellowship will be offered for a period of upto three years and covers travel expenses to the host institution.
- The host institution will be expected to provide the facilities needed for tuition fees, training, supervision and if possible free accommodation.

TO LAUNCH POST GRADUATE PROGRAMME

Training fellowships for women scientists in India at centers of excellence of in least developed countries

Purpose

The general purpose of the scheme is to institute fellowship programmes for female students who wish to pursue post graduate training's leading to a doctoral degree at the center of excellence in India and outside their own country. The general purpose of the scheme is to contribute to the emergence of a new generation of women leaders in science and technology, and to promote their effective participation in scientific and technological development of their countries.

The Specific Aim of the Schemes Are

- To improve access to educational and training opportunities in Science and Technology for young and talented women graduates.

- To increase scientific productivity and creativity of women scientists
- To empower new generation of talented women to assume a leadership role in science and technology and their application
- To sustainable development

Nature

- To enable them to pursue postgraduate studies leading to Ph.D. degree at centers of excellence either outside their country with in same region or in other regions.
- A candidate can either enroll as a full time research student in an institution outside her country and pursue part of her research at another institution in some other regions under a sandwich program.
- Each fellowship will be offered for a period of upped three years and covers travel expenses to the host institutions and a most living allowance, the amount of, which will be determined after consultation with the host institution.

The host institution will be expected to provide the facilities needed for tuition fees, training supervision, and if possible free accommodation

Host Institutions

Applicants should select renowned institutes outside their own country, preferably where they have already applied for post graduate admission of the precise field of proposed research and the country/region where the applicant would wish to pursue a post graduate research program.

Eligibility

The fellowships are open to qualified young women

graduates (generally less than 30 yrs. of age) from India and abroad.

The minimum qualifications of applicant is an M.Sc degree (or equivalent) or an outstanding B.Sc honours degree in any field of natural sciences.

Selection

- The fellowships are highly competitive and the selection will be based on scientific competence and merit.
- The applications will be reviewed by a panel of eminent scientists appointed by executive board.
- A limited number of fellowships (not exceeding twenty) will be provided to successful candidates for respective academic year.

FOR CREATIVE SERVICES (LINKING HIGHER EDUCATION FOR COMMUNITY SERVICE)

- To fill position in Information and creative services
- Tree scientists /horticulturists
- Regional coordinators
- Ecologists for the National Resource strategy and policy
- Leader of the ecosystem Rehabilitation programmes
- To prepare female entrepreneurs to face in the world of global changes
- Changing world market ; altering social structure, accelerating development in information technology
- Expanding industrialization
- Extending social services and education.

Mission for the Tasks

Enhance effective participation of women in industrial

development through promoting of women's ventures that efficiently utilize their potentials, skills and capabilities.

Tasks

- Provide technical and managerial assistance to female entrepreneurs through advisory services, guidance and industrial information.
- Training.
- Create effective coordinated programmes with other women.
- Support entities.
- Conduct studies and research.
- Promote self employment programmes.

International Center for Research Will Function

- To improve human welfare by reducing poverty, increasing cash income.
- Improving food and nutrition security.
- Enhancing ecosystem resilience in the tropics through improved agro-forestry systems.

ASIAN CENTER FOR HUMAN ECOLOGY

Mission-Strengthening and empowering individuals and families to interact effectively with their environments

Thrust Areas

- Human Ecology for Globalization.
- Partnership and networking.
- Restructuring the curriculum for linking higher education with community service to respond to the local needs for advancement/ evolution of Home Economics to Human Ecology.
- To gain insight from contacts between knowledge resources and socio-cultural realities in the entire

curricular system and for higher education, international cooperation/partnership for action, snaring their successful experience, technologies, materials, financial resources and learning for pilot studies on:

* Research and training for human resource development in on-farm, off-farm and non farm sectors, (concept of Home Management)
* Institutionalization of farm, off farm and non farm sectors for:
    - Case Studies on Conservation of Ecosystems.
    - Studies on Women, Agriculture and Rural Extension with special reference to Biodiversity (How families should avail these facilities).

- Setting priorities in research to help community in areas of agribusiness, biodiversity & Environment, non conventional energy systems and Human resource development.
- Promote Post Doctoral research and granting a]wards for strengthening its focus on rural life.
    * For incorporation of environmental considerations in their day to day activities.
    * The use of alternative and renewable energy resources.
    * Approaches that rely on market based incentive research creating conducive environments for voluntary, flexible and innovative actions and stimulating increased participation and commitment by all sectors of society.
    * To redefine the teaching-learning paradigm to create a technology-rich learning environment.

- Adult continuing Education and Extension:
    - Undergraduate, Post Graduate level courses in adult and continuing education/ non formal education
    - Certificate /diploma courses in adult education
    - Projects related to extension/field out reach and foundation course
    - Research documentation and publication to primary and secondary school models, low cost low technology models.
    - Application of modern technology suited to the open and distance education mode to reach out to all sections of our people.

Women's contribution is in fact very intensive and intimate in agriculture. It is not universally accepted that women were the first agriculturists; while men went out of hunting, women were envisaged in homestead cultivation as well as food gathering activities. Recent research suggests that it accounted for satisfying 80% of society food requirements. Women were also discovers of first tool of agriculture and it was they how started making baskets and earthen pots for storing foods. Ever since the beginning of civilisation women have played an important role in agriculture in almost every country of the world. In fact one cannot think of agriculture without women. There are as many women farmers in the world as men farmers. However with the passage of time and new technology inventions, the status of women in agriculture has undergone as sea change and they now play a subordinate role. They have lost all property rights and have little say in decision making.

The commissioner for scheduled castes and scheduled tribes submitted 28 reports (under article 338) on the working of the safeguards provided in the constitution of scheduled castes tribes.

Besides, the planning commission has set up on the eve of the commencement of each five-year plans, working group for the development and welfare of scheduled castes and scheduled tribes, apart from above institutions, several commission, committees have been set up by the Government of India and state governments from time to time, to go into the problems of the SCs and STs and also women and agricultural workers in general.

However, very scanty information is available with regards to the socio-economic status of scheduled caste women agricultural workers in the published material. However, efforts have been made to collect information as applicable-on agricultural labourers on one hand and scheduled caste women on the other, and to integrate the collated information into a meaningful whole.

It would not be absolutely irrelevant to mention that the socio-economic factor responsible for the poor wretched living a scheduled caste woman and agricultural workers in general, and then make observations, recommendations, with respect to the scheduled caste women in agriculture with in the available data information base.

In brief, the tribal women enjoy a better position than her counterpart in many tribal societies. However, the phenomenal changes occurring in the socio-economic field of the country affect the tribal women and tribal areas much more harshly than others.

In considering application of science and technology in tribal areas, focused consciously at tribal women would demand consideration of certain essential aspects relevant to their life and culture. To understand its ramifications and its impact role to play in the former than men. Her contribution to the economic well-being of a tribal family is crucial.

When dealing with tribal societies, as they are in our

country in the application of technological inputs, it might as well be appropriate that traditional attitudes and values give preeminence to authority and custom in the modulation of behaviour is recognised. It makes for stability and continuity of tradition. By the same token, it can also resist force of change and adaptation. Rationality or scientific temper based on authority but would accept as valid only those things of which evidences have been collected scrupulously. What is distinctive about the scientific methods is what is built into it, namely, the possibility of disproof. It is an adaptive, integrative, feedback process. Where inputs and new data, and new hypotheses as to what the underlying theories might be. If experiences an expectation differ either the body of scientific knowledge or the input hypotheses as to what the underlying feedback process where inputs are new data and new hypothesis or the data are refined or adjusted until observations and prediction can be brought back into agreement. We are not positing a kind of polarity between science and tradition but change and development can take place only if there is a willingness of examines previously held beliefs. Scientific knowledge does not postulate unconditional truths but thrush hypothesises valid for a range a specified conditions.

If these women are to be empowered as well we must start looking for a new vision, an alternative way of development:

- The person affected should be able to realise that the problem he faces is a legal problem and that a lawyer can help him.
- He must know where he can get such legal help.

The above two preconditions are markedly absent in our country and their absence would render any traditional legal service programme ineffective and deprive it of meaning, and utility.

Need of the Hour

- Short-term continuing education programmes dealing with specific aspects of law relevant to social, economic and political aspects of individual lives.
- Utilising existing curricular provisions to initiate profiles of injustice/victimisation.
- Setting up curriculum /learning materials, writers' groups to modify existing biases against the poor and oppressed.
- Study groups of experts examining existing development programmes as also persistent and recurrent problems (structural injustice) like floods, droughts, etc. and identifying legal aspects of implementation of social and economic development provision.
- Taking up socio-legal surveys and initiating socio-economic and legal action.

Our of six hundred and eighty-four million men and women in this country, only a very small number of persons are already aware of the laws. Even if the persons who can easily afford to purchase legal know-how are also discounted, it will still mean conscientisation of about five hundred million persons.

RACISM

The natural seminar on Racism in New Delhi on 11 Aug. 2001 made some suggestions and views that emerged increasing the level of literacy and awareness led to a better understanding of rights thereby reducing if not totally eliminating any form of discrimination. It was also opined that there was a need to increase the capacities of the people so that they know that their rights and duties are. Though untouchability has been abolished in the country it is still widespread in villages. Caste based exploitation becomes an instrument for the cause of legal literacy for people as a meaningful extension activity through a process of internal collaboration between departments of adults, continuing education and extension and the law colleges.

Trafficking in women is one of the worst form of violation of human rights — a form of modern day slavery where the victim is subjected to violence. Violation of personal integrity and total humiliation without any hope. The victim of such devastating violence may also end up with life threatening HIV/AIDS on a lifetime of human and personality disintegration. Trafficking is thus a violation of several human rights — among them, the very right to life, the right to liberty and security of person, the right to freedom from torture or cruelty, inhuman and degrading treatment, the right to home and family, the right to education and proper employment, the right to health care — everything that makes for a life with dignity.

Today, trafficking in women and children is one of the fastest growing areas of national and international criminal activity. It has created a complex criminal network at times, with the patronage of those in power. Lack of suitable laws and law enforcement machinery add to the problem. The term "trafficking" is most often used interchangeable with "prostitution". It is not widely known that prostitution, though at the case of trafficking is not the only form of trafficking, and even made children in addition to female children can be and are being trafficked by various nefarious purposes.

The problem of trafficking in women and children has received significant media coverage over the years. But the debate on its social legal and political aspects is still at the initial stage. The folder attempts academics, NGOs, National/ State Human Rights Institutions, civil servants, lawyers, media and UN agencies to bring forth various aspects of trafficking

— its forms the estimates, the causes, the consequences the modus operandi and role of national human rights commission (NHRC). The contents should in no way regarded as exploratory to indicate areas where much work needs to be done proper data needs to be gathered and solutions need to be debated worked out and made operational to eliminate caste-based discrimination by civilised society by increasing the level of literacy for better understanding the rights, addressing the issues of poverty, empowering the women in eliminating the caste based exploitation. So that caste being local problems could use vehicle of education to climb up the ladder of respectability and take up the issues and raising in international fame. When people form all castes should be encouraged in forming their view against racism.

The relevance to the issues of children living in a world with HIV/AIDS. It has changed the world in which all children live. Research has pointed out that women and children are increasingly becoming infected, with the majority of new infections in many parts of the world taking place in young people between the ages of 15 and 24. Younger children are predominantly infected and died world-wide, since the beginning of the epidemic infected by HIV positive mothers. Who are not aware of their infection and transmit the virus to the children before or during birth or through breast-feeding.

Adolescents are also highly vulnerable to HIV/AIDS and more so because their early sexual experiences often take place without access to proper information. The epidemic has also increased victimisation of children living in particularly different circumstances who are at a greater risk to infection, which in time leads to stigmatisation and greater discrimination. HIV/ AIDS is often seen primarily as a medical problem, while the holistic rights entered approach is more appropriate to tackle the much proader range of issues involved. Promotion and adaptation at national level of approaches inspired by the international guidelines of HIV/AIDS and human rights jointly issued by the office of United Nations high commissioner for Human Rights and the joint United Nation programmes on HIV/AIDS. States, programmes and agencies of the United Nation system as well as NGOs should contribute to the dissemination and implementation of guidelines. National human right commission in partnership with the national aid control organisation, societies, etc. to take up a right-based response to the HIV/AIDS epidemic within the country in close collaboration with civil society.

Human dignity is the quintessence of human rights. Trafficking of women and children both male and female is, for several nefarious activities. Prostitution, drug trafficking, organised crime and begging are some of them. Adoption of child and has become a mode of trafficking. Right of child universally acknowledged and also assumed in the constitution of India, recognise the 'right of development' as a basic right of every child. This requires rigid implementation of convention rights, on enabling environment which protects children from all kinds of discrimination and exploitation and the ending of social evils, such as child marriage, child labour. Coordinated action between parent and community and state is necessary. The information set to inform the society the magnitude of evil and mode of combating in societies involvement in the most effective means of combating social evil.

Trafficking encompasses all of the core and dust contentions part of trafficking women and children in is trafficking...only prostitution? Sexual slavery? Mail order brides? Organ trade? And bonded labour? Is trafficking always forced. Nature of the problem — why does trafficking takes place? For what? For who? For what are the women and children from India are regularly sent to Middle East. Girls in prostitution and bonded domestic service abroad and often tortured, held in imprisonment, sexual abused and raped.

Targets — poor women and children from socially and economically backward groups from rural areas and urban slums; adolescent, young girls and women sigmatised in society; unmarried/divorced separated/ widowed women; runaways/lost/abandoned/kidnapped/ abducted children; and ethnic minorities/SCs/STs/OBCs/ refugees/illegal migrants.

The Asia Pacific forum established in 1996 in Darwin Australia to promote dialogue committed to the growth of National Human rights in situations in the region supports through technical cooperation information dissemination and support. It also provides information on country based projects and on regional projects. Technical cooperation is provided to the forum members through common training and activities the objective being capacity building and upgradation of skills. National human right commission in India is an autonomous body set up under the protection of Human Rights Act, 1993 of the Indian Parliament to perform and undertake and promote research in the field of human rights through publications, the media seminars and other available means for the promotion of human rights, concerning population policies and trafficking within and across the national boundaries for the purpose of sexual exploitation, marriage, domestic work, or labour trade to combat trafficking coordinating and cooperation at national, local levels to review develop and strengthen comprehensive, essential and integrated strategies and measures so as to facilitate national/ local level agenda to set up a time frame and network with civil society. To coordinate with international organisations, working in the field, including UNICEF, NIFEM, UN centre for Human Right, BLO, UNESCO, UNDP, WHO, UNAID, UN Crime Prevention and Crime Justice Division, UNFPA, World tourism organisations, UN high commission for human rights to suggest strategies for implementation and to set up a time frame and network with the civil society to facilitate local national level agenda.

Trafficking in women and children as of not to pull and push. Industrialisation; urbanisation; poverty; deprivation low status of women and girls; lack of earning income opportunity; lack of alternate employment, disintegration of rural communities break down of joint family system; and erosion of social values; social conventions like dowry, polygamy, child marriage, etc., and a single status of women (unmarried, divorced, separated, widowed) create a platform for women's vulnerability. Desirability of easy life performed by consumerism, globalisation and liberalisation, which has served the traditional, social-economic fabric and have made the Indian women and children vulnerable, making their commodities in the market; lack of awareness about legal protection, and rights, lack of political will and corruption, lack of effective policing and law enforcement, lack of research and documentation for trafficking with and across the national boundaries.

Brief Overview

With the objective of ascertaining the views of all sections of society including academics, jurists, human rights activists, NGOs and other on the issue of Racism. Racial Discrimination, Xenophobia and Related Intolerance, as well as on issues relating to caste and race in India to combating all forms of discrimination irrespective of the label or nomenclature under which it occurs. The Commission's effort is to eradicate discrimination, wherever it is found. Thus, it did not really matter whether the discrimination fell under the label of caste, race, descent or any other category. None are acceptable.

The Chairperson reiterated the statement made by him at the Bangalore Seminar to the effect that the Commission had not formed its opinion on the issue of whether discrimination based on caste and race were co-terminous or similar, and that is would formulate its position only after the Public Consultations had taken place and the Commission had learnt the views of all concerned persons. He assured the gathering that the commission "had not mortgaged its mind to any preconceived notion or thought on the issue of racism," an issue which was being hotly debated. Justice Verma clarified that he had politely declined the invitation to participate in a Committee constituted by the Prime Minister to prepare for the World Conference for the obvious reason that would have been inconsistent with the autonomous character of the Commission. Additionally, he stressed that the NHRC formed its opinion only after taking into account the views of all concerned groups, howsoever diverse they might be.

It may be a

'small'....	'medium'.... or....	'large scale'
	NETWORK	
Traffics one woman/child at a time	Specialises in trafficking women/children from one specific country.	Recruits and/or sells women/children to the clientele.
	Keeps women/children under its control in clubs and brothels.	Very sophisticated network usually difficult to combat.
	Does not sell women/children but recruits them for clients.	Have easy access to fraudulent documents.
	Has political/economic/ national and international contacts.	Infrastructure in transit and distribution countries.
		Strong political/economic national/international contacts.

To make students professions and befitted in development departments for the effective enterprise development. We have to be risk taking and innovative in view of the dynamic changes of global liberalisation and making strategies and knowledge that improves daily lives of current and future generation.

To develop proficiency in students for planning, organising

and evaluating rural development programmes especially programmes for youth and women to be supported by field work and field projects examining the family as a significant ecosystem.

Management programmes explores design and function in conjugation with technology, user satisfaction and perception.

Relation with neighbouring countries and high on operand. However "India needs to focus on economic development now"

ORGANISE NATURALLY FOR BEST RESULTS IN STUDIES IN HIGHER EDUCATION

Science Attempts to Define the Nature of Reality

We make large promises to avoid making small presents. Those who are quick to promise are generally slow to perform globalisation for local action.

Biological systems are adaptable, resilient, and capable of generating perpetualness. Natural systems not only change, they change how they change. The challenge today for our organisations is to appreciate the "Strengths of natural systems, and design and operate to embrace their logics for globalisation of agriculture."

On course work, than the final thesis Ph.D. thesis is an area in need of further research and development.

THE ASIAN CENTRE FOR HUMAN ECOLOGY

(Resources, Newsletter and Events and Affiliates)

The Holistic Approach for Earth Ecosystem Studies for Conservation of Ecosystem, Towards Sustainable Communities

For the first time in history, nearly half of the world's people now live in urban areas characterised by human structures and activities.

Accreditation fosters excellence in education, encourages institutional improvement through continual self-study and evaluation, provides advice and assistance to established and developing institutions and protects institutions from encroachment that might endanger their educational effectiveness and academic freedom.

The Need and Importance of HRM in Higher Education

Educational is one of the most important factors in achieving development goals of the country. Higher education is of great significance for all-round development in a developing country like India. The number of quality of students coming out of its educational institutions shape a nation. The human resources at the collegiate level serve as the backbone of national development. The products of the colleges are the potential nation builder. The future scenario of political, social, cultural and economic sectors will depend on the contributions of the students of educational institutions today. Hence to attain national relevance and socio-economic viability in education the human resource factor has to be managed properly.

The assessment of HRM activity will provide clarity and focus on purpose, organisational credibility, pride and improved moral, as the staff knows what is expected of them and a goal to aim through specific targets. Hence it is important to evaluate the HRM in higher educational institutions.

In modern times personal management is one of the most complex and challenging fields of endeavour. Educational institutions are no exception to this general turned. On the other hand the management of human resources in educational institutions is more complex, because the quality of their teaching work is in no way going to affect the salary. Hence to generate maximum quality from the staff is more challenging in the field of education. Since the human resource is highly qualified, they expect a great extent of freedom in their field of work. The only possible way of increasing the efficiency of human resources is educational institutions are effective management by frequent evaluation and proper motivation mechanisms. The need of the hour is therefore a shift of focus to the people and to treat them with respect and dignity.

New Technologies

Chemical source of energy, Hydrogen energy, Geothermal energy, Alternate fuels for surface transport, urban and industrial waste and their conversion routes and industrial research and development.

Ministry of Non Conventional Energy Sources

India is fortunate to be endowed with an abundance of renewable energy sources These include biomass, sun, wind, ocean waters, urban and industrial wastes, hilly hydro and canal heads suitable for small and mini hydel sets, etc. The biomass includes large quantities of cattle dung and human excreta, agricultural residues, bagasse and other by-products of agro-based industries like paper mills etc. The potential of some of these is indeed enormous as indicated in the next page table.

TABLE

Estimated Potential for Renewable Energy Technologies in India

Sources / Systems	*Approx. Potential*
Biogas plants (No.)	12 million
Improved woodstoves (No.)	120 million
Biomass	17,000 MW
Solar energy	20 MW/sq.km
Wind energy	20,000 MW
Small hydro power	10,000 MW
Ocean energy	50,000 MW

There are an estimated 232 million cattle in the country and if one-third of the dung produced annually from these is available for production of biogas and for recycling as farm manure, 12 million biogas plants can be installed. Against this potential, cumulative total of 27.65 lakh family type and toilet-linked plants under the National Project on Biogas Development and 2360 plants under the Community, Institutional and Nightsoil based Biogas Plants Programme have been installed up to December 1998.

Another major programme relates to promotion of solar thermal technologies. Among these, solar water heating systems occupy an important place. Hot water is needed for a number of applications at homes, in offices, institutions, hotels, hospitals, industrial units etc. The Ministry's promotional efforts have resulting in the installation of 4,50,000 sq.m. of solar water heating collectors which can heat more than 22 million litres of water to a temperature of 60-70 degrees C everyday. This is no small achievement and the technology of solar water heating is now fairly mature even though there may be scope for some improvements. The advantages of using solar water heating systems are quite obvious. Use of 1000 domestic solar water heaters of 100 litre capacity each will contribute to a peak load having of 1 MW. Use of huge systems, can result in substantial saving of electricity or other commercial fuels like coal, wood, furnace oil etc. Besides this, carbon dioxide emissions into the atmosphere can be prevented. According to a conservative estimate, the potential in our country for deployment of such systems is around 30 million sq.m. of collector area, against which 4.5 lakh sq.m. of collectors have been installed. This brings out the enormous scope that still exists in this area of renewable energy. In recent years, the manufacturing base of solar water heating systems has improved substantially and there are 37 approved manufacturers with production capacity of 100000 sq.m. of collector area per year. Large-scale promotion of solar water heating systems, through a number of financial and fiscal incentives, has been taken up. Besides the Indian Renewable Energy Development Agency (IREDA), five banks have come forward to provide soft loan for those interested.

A notable feature of the wind power programme has been the interest envinced by private entrepreneurs in setting up commercial wind power projects. In fact, of the 1000 MW capacity created so far, 950 MW has been established in commercial projects while the remaining 50 MW has been contributed by demonstration projects. IREDA has set up a revolving fund to finance commercial projects and has received assistance by way of sizable credit form multilateral and bilateral aid agencies like World Bank, GEF, DANIKA, KFW, and OECF (Japan).

Biomass as a source of electricity holds considerable promise. It is estimated that 405 million tones of crop residues are produced every year, a large portion of which goes waste or is used inefficiently. By using only the surplus biomass materials for the monitoring and evaluation support to be given to the adult education programmes.

Rural Development

Except a few institutions which have taken keen interest in rural development, the universities in general have ignored the aspect. The Agricultural Universities have had a limited focus and perspective of covering only few aspect of rural development and seldom treated its rural development activities with an integrated approach.

The Universities have to seriously plan low cost alternatives in upgrading knowledge levels, employable skills, and attitudes conducive to people's participation in development. While the Universities visualise a co-ordinating/ initiating role in this regard, colleges as grass-root units of higher education can undertake meaningful field work within the context of a scheme/ programme.

The Department of Adult, Continuing Education and Extension could become a nodal agency to act as a bridge between the departments of studies and the rural communities by promoting programmes of continuing and community education in every branch of learning with emphasis on the following functions :

- Creation and dissemination of knowledge.
- The development of human resources.
- The management and implementation of projects.
- Creating usable literature for integrated rural development.

Environmental Education

The role of education in the ambit of environmental problems and opportunities is a crucial one. Environmental Education should be integrated as part of the system of formal education at all levels to provide necessary knowledge understandings, values and skills.

Establishment of Asian Centre for Human Ecology at Delhi University

To generate awareness and to enable handling the problems of environment, the education system needs to be revamped.

The curricula could be horizontal embracing all the related subjects or vertical dialing with one package covering the ecological social cultural and other aspects of particular problem, it is inherently interdisciplinary in character. It should be relevant to the problems at home and must help learners to acquire knowledge values and skills necessary to help solve the problems. Environmental education involves learning from the environment as well as about the environment and require changes in the established methods of teaching especially in formal education. With the adoption of this problem oriented and action oriented approach environment becomes a continual and forward looking affair.

Objectives. To create a comprehensive data base.

To strengthen the use of gender analysis in research and technology development to ensure that women's as well as men's agriculture enterprises are fully considered for defining research programmes and setting priorities. To develop training modules and imparting training and publication of manuals for sensitising gender related issues in research programmes and policy development.

- To develop and test women specific models of technology transfer that are to be promoted through regular extension agencies by collaborating with SAUS/ ICAR institutes.
- To promote women specific technology for reducing drudgery on women in forming operations including post harvest and home management.
- To provide leadership and sponsor training programmes in order to strengthen the knowledge and skill related to gender implications informing system approach for researchers and extension personnel and to provide consultancy service within and outside the country on women specific programmes for research/projects and development.
- To prepare video films and other publicity material on improved equipments/technologies and allied activities for extension work. To establish the Asian Centre for Human Ecology at Delhi University, has multidisciplinary faculty and experienced and trained man power in the area of rural development, human resource development, conservation of ecosystem. The faculties of Arts and Social Sciences and Mathematical Sciences offer Bachelor of art

B.A. Vocational studies, Bachelor of Commerce, Bachelor of library and information science. And faculty of science in Home science, Nursing, and science and pharmacy, the faculty of Music and fine arts offer Bachelor of Arts, (Hons.) in Music, Fine Arts, painting, sculpture, applied art, print making, photography, History of art. The other faculty of education and faculty of technology all offer Bachelor degree examinations and degrees recognised by the Delhi University. However, the certificate diplomas in the faculty of science/Arts/ social sciences & Mathematical Sciences and postgraduate diploma course in Tourism and postgraduate diploma in Book Publishing and international marketing. One year postgraduate certificate & post control and analytical methods in chemistry & biochemistry, health education, immunology and allergy, medical radio-diagnosis dermatology & verneology.

The diploma course in health education under the faculty of Medical Sciences shall be under the Dean of Faculty of medical sciences. Every candidate seeking admission to diploma course in health education shall have the Master's degree in selected social sciences (*i.e.,* psychology/sociology/ anthropology/social work/economics/political science or education or nursing from recognised universities with at least one years experience in community health welfare programme or teaching in social/biological sciences/physical education/ home science. Preference will be given to those candidates who are in service.

The course of study shall be the scope of papers :

English : Paper A & B; *Physical Paper a & b,* Biology paper (a) Botany paper, (b) Zoology. English shall be the medium of examination in all the subjects provided the candidates will have the option to give them answers to questions in

Hindi in respect to the following optional subjects : Economics, History, Commerce, Geography, Civics, Deductive logic, Inductive logic, Psychology, Mathematics.

Women, Environment and Development

An attempt is made to outline women's role in the management of their environment and the impact of policies, or the lack of integrated and ecologically sound policies, on their work roles and status. In this context, government and NGO responses to ecological needs and therefore related women's needs, briefly reviewed.

Gender Justice for Progress

A study of the process and factors that have shaped the progress of the status of woman, reveals a deliberate and organic relationship between emancipation of women and the true facets of development. A brief survey of the areas of women's health, education, economic status and social and political empowerment indicates that nation's prosperity is directly proportional to the progress of women.

Women's Health

The health of Indian women is intricably related to the socio-economic status of the household and their age and kinship/marital status within the households. Given the predominantly patriarchal set-up, women and girls get a lesser share in the intra-household distribution of health goods and services, compared to men and boys. However, in the intra-households distribution of labour, women get the major share of economic, procreative and family responsibility. Due to the competing demands on their time and energy as well as their socialisation, women tend to neglect their health. Statistics indicate that education and employment of women have resulted in reduction of fertility rates. Female literacy postpones child birth, and helps in fewer and healthier children.

Education for Women

In India, the gap between boys and girl's participation in education is the quintessential symbol of the girl-child

To generate awareness and to enable handling the problems of environment, the educational system needs to be revamped. The curricula could be horizontal embracing all the related subjects, or vertical dealing with one package. The relevance of the two approaches will depend on the particular situation ensuring side by side that there is no mis-match between developmental priorities.

Continuing education in the area of environmental sciences and technology to cater the group of teachers, scientists, technologists and others who had no opportunity to learn about environment during their school and college days is becoming popular.

The educational process in this regard underlines certain stages :

- Awareness supported by information (both descriptive and scientific),
- Appreciation of activities by others in terms of environmental advocacy and action,
- Formulation of the stage of the local environmental problem,
- Initiating preventive action immediately, and
- Participation in the process of area-development and people-development planning.

Towards this end, the following base is required :

— Base data relating to each environmental concern;
— Basic data about specific development plans;
— Development models/perspectives guiding such plans; and

— Information pertaining to the implementational agencies / personnel.

Legal Literacy

The cause of legal literacy for the people as a meaningful extension activity by the university system has been championed through a process of internal collaboration between departments of adults, continuing education and extension and the law colleges and external collaboration with various governmental agencies and social action groups.

The success of the traditional legal service programme and society marked by integrated power of physical, emotional, dynamic, intellectual, ethical, aesthetic and spiritual potentialities for universal upliftment.

Frontiers of knowledge, age, therefore, bond to expand unimaginably and new researches will oblige humanities sciences, technologies and fire arts to arrive at new equations and new combinations. Development in communication information and technology will open up new and cost effective approaches for providing the reach of higher education for meeting the demands of explosion of information, fast changing nature of occupations and life long education.

India has been in the forefront of all global initiatives that have communicated in the philosophy of human ecology. The scientific expertise to increase the relevance of higher education by making courses more oriented. To enhance empowerment in human resource with special emphasis on education the disciplines of agri-business, biodiversity and environment, biotechnology, non-conventional energy system have been merged to make a unified field of Human ecology for systematic vision of the strategic issues like :

- Perspectives of higher education for community empowerment in human ecology.

- Education extension and outreach updating the climics with special reference to Home Science.
- Prioritisation of research agenda in Agribusiness, Biodiversity and Environment, Biotechnology, Non-conventional Energy systems.
- Institutionalisation for action for Human Resource Development.

Preservation of the environment and conservation of researches such as fossil fuel and water is a matter of international concern. Action that threatened survival of various aspects of plants and animals, created renewed interest in ecology, the science concerned with interrelationships between organism and environment both organic and inorganic.

The Meaning of Research

Human beings one unique products of their emotion and evolution in contrast to other forms of animal life:

- Education and development programmes to involve women right from grass-root level.
- To coordinate network of regional and national centres and to provide a forum for gathering and dissemination of information on experiences and findings of those in the field.
- To facilitate the entry of women into employment in the field of science and technology and their progress within such employment.
- To deal effectively with global development issues and opportunities to broaden their perspectives.
- Training and award programmes to support activities to meet both needs ultimately leading to the production of critical mass of experienced trained researchers for global, sustainable equitable development.

CHAPTER-8

CENTERS OF EXCELLENCE

Observations from which a hypothesis is derived (inductive reasoning). Then the researcher proceeds deductively to determine the consequences that one to be expected if the hypothesis is true. Data are then collected through the inductive method to verify, reject, or modify the hypothesis. Thus the researcher is continually moving back and forth between the inductive methods of observation and data collection and the deductive method of hypothesizing the anticipated consequences of events.

Science. The term science may be thought of an approach to the gathering of knowledge rather than field of subject matter. Science, put simply consists of two primary functions : (1) the development of theory and (2) the testing of substantive hypothesis that are deduced from theory. The scientist, therefore, is engaged in the use, modification and/or creation of theory. The scientists begins with a set of ideas that direct the effort and with the goal that entails the development of testing theory.

By attempting to apply the rigorous, systematic observation and analysis used in physical and biological sciences to area of social behaviour, the social science have grown and have advanced humanity's knowledge of itself. The field of anthropology, economics, education, political science, psychology and social anthropology have become recognised as science by any authorities. To the extent that these fields are founded on scientific methodology, they are sciences. Some reject the concept still defining science in terms of subject matter rather than methodology. Historically their position can be readily explained. Since scientific methods were first used in investigation of physical phenomena, tradition has identified science with physical world. Only within the last century has the methodology of science in terms of subject matter rather than methodology.

Because human value is so complex it is much more difficult to develop sound theories of human behaviour than to predict occurrences in the physical world, research on human subjects has numerous problems.

Today we live in a world that has benefited greatly by the progress made by the biological and physical sciences, infant mortality is decreasing, and life expectancy continues to increase. But progress towards a sustainable future has simply been too slow.

A regional and participatory process was used to produce analysis of environmental impact of alternative development scenarios and policy action will be included in the further GEO report as well as more extensive analysis of current policy responses, their impact, and the reasons for their success and failures. The introduction of these elements in the continuous GEO assessment has already started. As a result several countries report marked progress in curbing environment pollution and showing the rate of resource degradation as well as reducing the intensity of resource use.

Internationally Agenda in 1922 in Rio de Janeirno provides the global consensus on the road map towards sustainable development. UNEP continues to be the environmental voice of United Nations responsible development, scientific analysis monitoring and assessment. Increasingly, United Nation Organisations, the World Bank and regional banks are "greening" their programme. New approaches to international policies are being developed, tested and implemented.

Collaborative arrangements: With the network of institutions on JNU campus like Institute of Mass Communication, The Indian Council of Social Science Research Campus will substantially promote networking amongst scientists and cater to each other needs.

Education for Extension

Linkages for economic status and social power :

- Greater economic efficiency of production technologies to the need for location specifically, social acceptability and environment sustainability.
- To generate new knowledge for information based technologies to strengthen means of dissemination needed to transmit this information to farmers.
- Optimisation in the management by producers of their available resources, sustainability, coping with diversity, by adopting technology.
- To make information transfer more cost effective, in communication, between researchers, extensionists and their farmer clients for effective learning.
- Teach to know what makes both teaching and learning effective for the establishment of a variety of rural services.
- To bring desirable changes in the behaviour of concerned persons through educational methods to improve their general standard of living with their own efforts.
- Educational methods aimed at the dissemination of knowledge leading to systematic learning make process of development a continuous process as a discipline of formal education as informal education.
- To change the attitude and practices of the people with whom he work is done in agriculture, and

home economics, for home making or bring about continuous improvement in their physical economic and social well-being through individual and cooperative efforts.

To have close relationship of the discipline with technical sciences and social sciences for the needs importance and techniques for cooperative extension work for action programmes?

Objectives

- To update and modify the undergraduate course curriculum in collaboration with ICAR Division with Deans of Faculties of agriculture, agricultural engineering, dairy technology, home science, horticulture, fisheries and forestry.
- Implementation of revised curriculum in all SAU's and Universities under UGC for new courses on computer application, Biodiversity, Biotechnology, Principles of Ecology, Agribusiness Management, marketing and environmental sciences for improvement and assurance of quality education.
- Resource Centre for outreach activities :

  - Working with communities for conducting need based studies, survey, adaptive research, development, field trials, demonstrations and dissemination of appropriate technologies amongst the niral poor.
  - Networking in innovations, participation, and demonstrations at national and international level.
  - Popularisation of new technologies and designed to test technologies, for the specific geographical areas.
  - Linkages and interaction with national and

state level science and technology institutes in technology adaptation and exchange.

- Creation of assets/infrastructure to utilise locally available human resource to facilitate implementation of action oriented projects for impact assessment, training facilities, workshops, laboratories, tools and equipment in the areas and generation of matching solutions, conducting training programmes
- Conducting need-based studies, survey, adaptive research and development, field trails, dissemination of appropriate technologies amongst rural poor. Popularisation of new need based research upto commercialisation in agricultural sciences/home sciences, basic sciences for academic excellence in the area of postgraduate education.

— Balancing Higher education for community service:

- For better management of human and environment to improve people's life and environment in the view of rapid technological advancement and community belonging to the poorest of the poor families.
- *Earth eco system research :* To mobilise community support in understanding, promoting and enabling better child care through education.
- To provide supportive services through education, women's development programmes such as safe drinking water, environmental sanitation, pre school education below 6 years.

Automation and computerisation touch every aspect of

our lives reducing our physical labour and increasing our leisure time. The splitting of the atom, space travel and developments in the field of electronics such the laser, super conductivity and silicon chip, promise improvements and adventures that are beyond the scope of most people imagination science for meeting the challenges of a college science course. In expensive supplement offers students practical guidelines for recycline and conserving energy.

Science Popularisation

Man is an important element of the environmental complex. His activities growing population, industrial and human settlements, social religious and economic set ups are posing newer ecological problems. Understanding his ecological role the anthropologists, sociologists, psychologists, economists demographers supply data to persons working on human ecology. To be acquainted with various disciplines of physical and biological sciences in order to get integrated picture of the environmental complex in relation to organic world. In order to quantify his data an ecologist has to collect information which could be subjected to mathematical formulation for precise communication to other working in the field.

Indian culture is deeply rooted in two different but intricate traditions. In India rethinking has begun. More and more of the scientists, artists, scholars have started looking into their rich traditions. A large number of NGO's and voluntary agencies have now entered the value education in India. Some of them have evolved innovative programmes.

Home science, in reality is deeply and closely related to life. A model home science curriculum world, therefore, care to cover all such factors, fields, and interests which affects a person's development, his life, in the family and in the community. A change to meet the challenges and opportunities of today's higher education enter. Today higher education enterprise an immensely broad based discipline full of rich academic vocational and professional elements which need to be exploited to the fullest extent in future educational needs.

Professional courses would provide under spectrum of experience of graduating students hence sufficient weightage on:

- Nutrition and health education by the community the referral services in expectant and nursing mothers, and women in age group of 15 to 45 years.
- In partnership with DARE for effective linkages at the national and international level and partnership among different ministries organisations within the country.

HUMAN ECOLOGY FOR BIODIVERSITY AND ENVIRONMENT

International Centre for Partnership and Linkages with Dare

To provide additional support for training of the faculties and infrastructure development of social sciences and policy includes studies for technology assessment refinement and transfer. The research extension linkages to strengthen and integration of technology assessment and refinement programmes for :

- Front-line demonstrations including farmers
- Action programme pertaining to institute village linkage programme.
- Research centre for women agriculture rural extension for the development of appropriate farming system research.
- To test promising varieties in tribal and hill region

for adaptation of agro-pastoral systems in hill terrain for valley and hilly areas of Uttaranchal.

- Technology dissemination in innovations with revised curriculum for SAUs.
- Development of training programmes with the centres of advanced studies — the pre-service and in-service training in educational technologies in emerging areas for the development of professional competence for broadening the concept of Home Science to Human Ecology.

Effective linkages at the national and international levels and partnership among different ministry organisations within the country is the need of the hour. Agriculture sector has delivered goods to the country for sustainable and economic reform.

The emerging demand are to be met through increased productivity, sustainability, environmental and ecological security profitability and competitiveness in the backdrop of decline in factor productivity, loss of biodiversity natural resource shrinkage degradation, climate change, intensifying completion in the international trade and widening economic disparities. The challenges are formidable yet within our reach. If the opportunities are harnessed in the interest of small and marginal farmers on the resource scarce situation so that large number of small and disadvantaged farmers are benefited and the efforts to achieve doubling of food production and eradication of poverty can be set in motion. To plan coordinate undertake aid promote and coordinate education research and its application in agriculture agro forestry, animal husbandry, fisheries, home science and allied sciences. Instituting and promoting transfer of technology programmes to look into the problems of broader areas of rural development concerning agriculture by developing cooperative programmes. To include human resources development, commensurate with new challenges and opportunities both at national and global level, for the holistic advancement in agriculture and allied subjects while ensuring optimal use of natural resources in partnership with all stakeholders especially the state with all stakeholders especially the state agriculture universities (SAUs), farmers, NGOs and promote sector etc. To achieve national objectives of poverty alleviation and welfare of disadvantaged and weaker section of the society. However, our production of agri horticulture crops has secured a prestigious position with Indian being second largest producer of rice, wheat fruit and vegetables in the world.

In order to maintain our biodiversity and broadening the genetic base by having improved varieties to increase production. To sensitising partners about its plans and programmes. The project Human Ecology for biodiversity and environment has three major components: (1) agro-ecosystem research in research programmes, (2) Innovations in technology dissemination under which technology dissemination and (3) priority-setting monitoring and evaluation to develop mechanism for priority setting, monitoring and evaluation of the project.

For partnership and linkages include International linkages through memorandum of understanding with Director South Campus, University of Delhi to sign MOU with DARE for the establishment of Centre for Biodiversity and Environment.

To undertake long term research agenda to bring research and knowledge to the community, human ecology combines the interests theories and studies of geographer, ecologists, and anthropologists to include in the undergraduate and postgraduate courses. This will require the links of environmental education organisations. It will be in the interest of botanists, plant ecologists, and conservation biologist resource managers for the management of various ecosystems. This can be combined with the departments of Home Science which will offer both masters and doctoral graduate programmes. The programmes which focuses on management of work place environments and historical preservation in conjunction with technology, user satisfaction and perfection of work and residential environments.

The international research and emphasis on international will provide advance knowledge and understanding of specialised fields. These may require the collateral course work where background is inadequate.

The grants and the projects under consideration by international agencies can support for such courses under exchange programme.

MISSION

- For institution strengthening and linkages for research capacity building in collaborative programmes in research and training.
- To promote participation in education to bring into sharp focus the central role of human development, into poverty reduction.
- To promote behaviour studies with practical application of knowledge across the domains of research, outreach and international programmes.
- For empowering and strengthening families and individuals in addressing the challenges of opportunities in their environments.
- To promote scholarships, and initiative that enhance the positive development of individuals, and families, address the problem that concerns of families in the community and acknowledge the diversity of families and community served by the college.
- To encourage scholarly efforts across the broad mission of the college/institute of Home Science/ Human Ecology.

INTERNATIONAL CENTRE FOR HUMAN ECOLOGY FOR BIODIVERSITY AND ENVIRONMENT

Objective — Setting priorities in Agribusiness

Providing educational programmes to respond to human needs by improving nutrition and health, advancing environmental design and technology, promoting human development and securing economic and social well-being for individuals.

Drivers. Rural Development, Human Resource Development, Promotion of educational and economic interest for all sections of society, Multinational collaborations for building, scientific and academic community by linking with partners, Networking to increase and contribute to International research.

It will combine the interests, theories and studies of : Geographers, Ecologists, Anthropologists, Home Economists/ consumer Science Specialists, Psychologists, Agriculture Scientists, Economists and Biologist

Centres

- Asian Centre for Human Ecology
- International Centre for Bio-diversity and Environment
- Other National Centres

Projects

- Conservation of Ecosystem of Central Himalayas with special reference to Gola Catchment area — A case study of conservation of hill community.
- International Centre for Human Ecology for :
  - — building a successful community through education to empower themselves and their families.

— knowledge, technological advances.

- To bring knowledge through their programmes to have access to the latest research and recommendations meaningful to the community.

Countries in Alliance. Austria, Netherlands, Germany, France, Italy, Mexico, Russia, China.

To meet the long term goal of human resource development with reference to in service and prospective graduates in the light of women in agriculture and rural extension there is a need to impart relevant education and training to young men and women for managing income generating and development activities on behalf of rural urban and slum producers.

We have to be very precise about the goal of developing links to build bridges between researchers and extension workers should not make us forget that specialisation and division of labour have contributed to growth throughout history. Sometimes a bit of competition between different sectors will lead to improved performance by each of them as long as social and institutional goals are clear. Working with constraints and responsibility is sheer drudgery, but from another point of view it is the most challenging task that a women can ever undertake.

FOR THE CAUSE OF LINKAGES

National. To implement most of its programmes through the ICAR Institutes, Research organisations, NGOs with whom it has strong linkages. These linkages will be further nurtured and strengthened by its fellows in the projects and Institutions.

International. To promote collaborative activities in the areas of agricultural research for modalities of cooperation. To establish bilateral linkages with Foreign universities for development and modification of course curricula at Post Graduate and Under Graduate level

Overseas training. Education technology for outreach training programmes.

Collaboration with the Universities of USA

Texas A & M University: To develop the human resources; faculty exchange for institutional capacity building in the areas of evaluation methodology; ecosystems; meat processing technology; skill development for Agribusiness education.

Collaboration with ISNAR for research training in the various disciplines of agriculture and management of research, joint collaborative projects and; study visit in respect of scientist and scholar for international linkage for Human Resource Development with special reference to Agriculture Rural Extension and other institutions for training on pre-service and in-service graduates.

ICAR CENTRE FOR HUMAN ECOLOGY-UNIVERSITY OF DELHI

It is my fond hope that this centre shall help individuals and agencies involved in a development work. And activism in realising the dream for better eco-friendly humane and sustainable society by travelling on the road which is less travelled.

Background

The project entitled "Studies on popularisation on mushrooms through "training programmes" has organised a "Congress on Human Ecology for Women" to include human resource development and technology assessment and refinement as new paradigm for holistic advancement in agriculture and allied subjects.

The students are alive to the expectation of society and their role in the changing world order. To bring in sharp focus the issues are :

- Strengthening relations with equal environment work cooperatively. To commensurate with new challenges and opportunities both at the national and global with public and private institutions, legislative bodies industry, state and community organisations and other units in the university.
- Close linkages of faculty and students with the real world.

METHODOLOGY

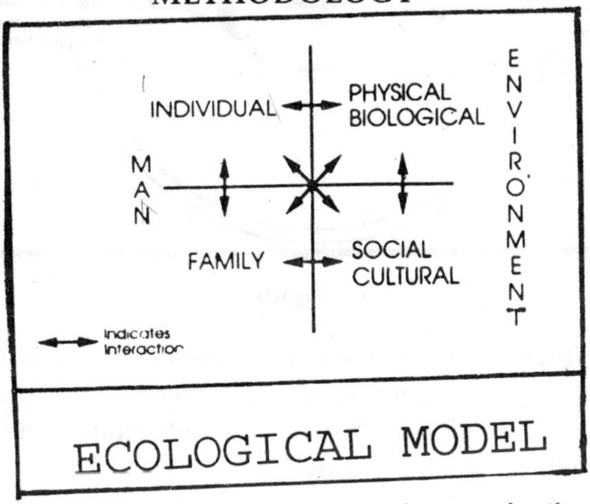

Figure: Ecological system model in totality focus on family ecology

Center for Human Ecology will function ecologically emphasizing collective efforts to achieve a critical mass of knowledge and activity,energizing the field and contributing to a better quality of life of all. It will be the combination of scholarly productivity and modeling.

Farm household system in Indian rural setting consists of the following subsystems which are closely interlinked and inter active

- household as decision making unit
- farm, off farm and non farm activities

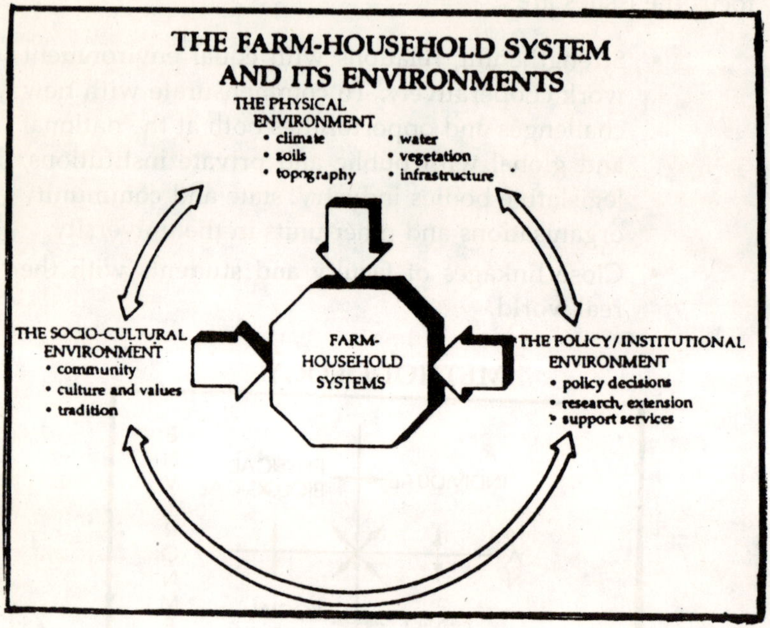

Figure

Productive by coupling the older general disciplines of humanities, social sciences and commerce to their applications in the new economy and having adequate fields based experience to enhance knowledge with kills and develop appropriate attitudes.

International Cooperation

With the increased development of transport and communication, the, global village is witnessing a growing emphasis on international cooperation and higher education is one of them. India has been in the forefront to adopt the new information society technologies such as distance education and internet to forestall the further widening of the gap between itself and the advanced countries, international cooperation in education is seen in this context of partnership- rather than air- where countries assist each other by sharing their successful experience as technologies, material and financial resources and learning to appreciate each other's cultural heritage.

Visionxs and Tasks Ahead

Towards a new synthesis:

In this new age, great cultural achievements of the past have to be recovered and enriched in the context of the contemporary advancement. Our legacy of innovative programmes provided a nurturing culture for significant programs that have serves to improve the human conditions. Today human ecological philosophy provides the context for developing serving individuals. To record the legacy of past, adoption of social cultural and technological changes and present vision for future.

NODAL CENTRE FOR HUMAN ECOLOGY

Financial Mechanism

For the projects for the development of infrastructure for

- Relevance of education
- Promoting of excellence and quality in education
- Equity and access for management of higher education and UGC administration for "Financial Mechanism"

Education develops man power for different levels of economy and empowers the poor masses to become self-reliant enough to participate in the process of nation development.

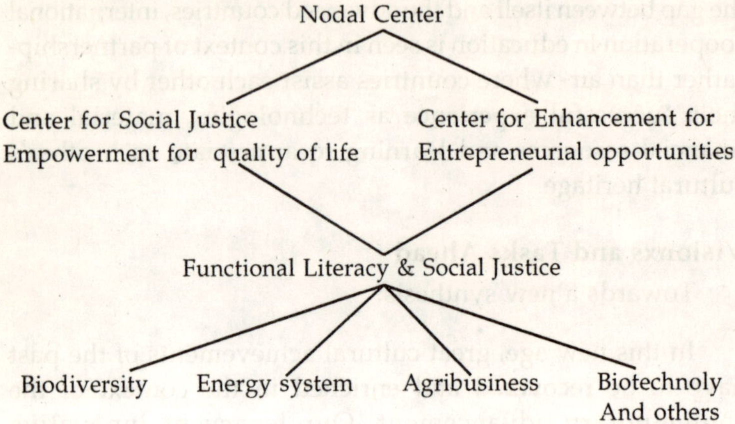

MULTI-LEVEL APPROACH

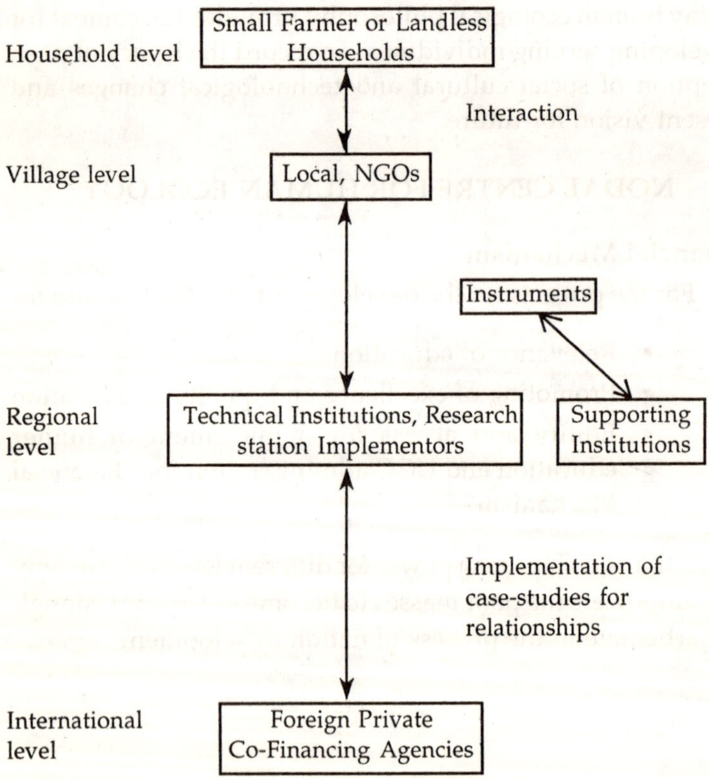

The main objectives of the proposed center will be

- To identify various target groups of human ecology for women as well as those who are to be trained in imparting and in developing the field of human ecology and consequent.
- To review currently employed teaching methods and assess how far these are suitable, and what appropriate methods and training programmes need to be devised.

METHODOLOGY

RESEARCH	EXTENSION		EDUCATION
Module-1 Pre-feasibility	Module-II Feasibility	Module-III Implementation	Module-IV Impact
Physical Environment	Identification of target population	Action based	An associative economy supporting
Climate Soils Topography Water Vegetation Infrastructure	Identification of economic activities/ farming system Resource mobilisation and provision Management consultancy Linkage building with third party	Participatory Multi level	the poor Rate of adoption Income generation Dietary awareness
Policy/Institutional Environment	Process extension and movement building		
Policy decision Research, extension Support services	Monitoring and ongoing self evaluation Marketing		
Socio Cultural Environment			
Community Culture and values Tradition			

COLLABORATIONS

1. Village Level

(i) Gram Panchayat
(ii) Van Panchayat
(iii) Fruit Utilization Department
(iv) Local NGOs

2. National Level

(i) G.B. Pant University, Pantnagar
(ii) Departments of Delhi University, Delhi
(iii) Kumaon University, Nainital
(iv) Forest Research Institute, Dehradun
(v) Indian Council of Agriculture Research Center, Almora
(vi) G.B Pant Institute of Himalayan Environment & Development

3. International Level

(i) Texas A & M University, Texas
(ii) Texas Agriculture Extension Services, College Station, Texas
(iii) Michigan State University, Michigan
(iv) College of Human Ecology, Michigan State University, Michigan

- Interrelations between the various components of human eco-system with the planning and principles.

Strategic Planning

- Improve access to quality education and expert knowledge.
- Achieve more active learning.

- Generate new knowledge and scholarship across mission.
- Promote problem solving to address for society needs.
- Advance diversity within community.
- Make people *matter*.

Future Planning for Action Points

- Expansion of research and outreach with people, resources and facilities.
- Postgraduate degree/diploma programmes for pre-service, in-service graduates.
- Other training programmes — short-term and doorstep (tailor programmes as per need)
- Research and training programme for wiring the curriculum of school and university

For the Considerations of Policy Makers, Dealing with National and International Concern on Management

To meet the long term goal of human resource development with reference to in-service and perspective graduates in the light of women agriculture and rural extension there is a need to impart relevant education and training to young men and women for managing income generating and development activities on behalf of rural urban and slum producers.

We have to be very precise about the goal of developing links to build bridges between researchers and extension workers should not make us forget that specialisation and division of labour have contributed to growth throughout history. Some times a bit of competition between different sectors will lead to improved performance by each of them as long as social and institutional goals are clear. Working with constraints and responsibility is sheer drudgery, but extension, Home Science and Nutrition. Sustainable and/equitable use of agro-biodiversity.

- Eco development concerns in Natural agricultural farming system, R&D approaches.

To meet the emerging demands for- productivity, sustainability, and environmental and ecological security. To coordinate research with the community perception education and reforms.

CHAPTER 9

CONCLUSION

The psyche of Indian parents needs to be changed. Instead of forcing them children to concentrate only on academies they should encourage them to develop their talent and give them the freedom to pursue into personal freedom. It should be judged on the basis of their performance. Our greatest challenge is to give power of scale to our farmers. India has the agri-cultivation to grow any thing. His focus: encouraging live stock ownership to empower rural human and get labour of the farm. He hopes to push for private participation in rural infrastructure development and the food claim arrangement. It is all a matter of getting the right idea at the right place the right time in the rural economy.

Basically the small Indian farmer is a reluctant and lazy farmer, village labour force moving to towns in the off-season and returning back in the sowing and harvesting season. This is a regular feature in the hill villages. Hence even if the transfer of technology was done at the grassroots level and man to man needs were tried to be achieved, it is not necessary that the farmers will continue with the process. The basic nature is thus a constraint in ensuring their further participation, once the projects ended and the inputs were withdrawn. Although, by this stage the farmers were trained to generate the inputs as well as channelise the marketing, they did little to further the work. Whilst the same was being managed by the project, it was fine with them.

The projects have bridged major communication gaps, and have succeeded in transfer of Science and Technology at grassroots level to the women within their resources and environment. The findings/observations of the projects provide broad guidelines for government and NGOs for planning and implementation of projects at State and National levels. The finding can be utilised effectively by other research organisations to further enhance the work areas. The students also benefit as the case studies provide a base for work towards achievement of higher education. On the international level the projects can serve as a model for a sustainable life style as we move towards the 21st Century especially in regard to socially weak the rural poor women Indian culture is deep rooted in the different but intricate traditions. In India rethinking has begun. More and More of scientists, artists scholars have started looking into their rich traditions which were lost. These should be integrated approach in the value oriented education, national integration and international understanding etc. They should be handed in a comprehensive manner under the broad spectrum of social responsibility and inner development of human personality. A large number of NGO's and voluntary agencies have now entered the value education in India. Some of them have evolved innovative programmes particularly in the area of environmental education to bring about an eco-development person, the right path of development with a curricular area in which the need and interest of the children could be met through a focus on the local environment. Students must be given an opportunity to develop a sense of "ownership" and 'empowerment' so that they are fully invested and motivated to became responsible active citizen.